D1462279

Why Sovereignty Matters

DATE DUE

Why Sovereignty Matters

Jeremy Rabkin

The AEI Press

Publisher for the American Enterprise Institute

WASHINGTON, D.C.

1998

Available in the United States from the AEI Press, c/o Publisher Resources Inc., 1224 Heil Quaker Blvd., P.O. Box 7001, La Vergne, TN 37086-7001. To order, call toll free 1-800-269-6267. Distributed outside the United States by arrangement with Eurospan, 3 Henrietta Street, London WC2E 8LU, England.

ISBN 0-8447-7117-1

1 3 5 7 9 10 8 6 4 2

THE AEI PRESS
Publisher for the American Enterprise Institute
1150 17th Street, N.W., Washington, D.C. 20036

Printed in the United States of America

Contents

Preface

International law has acquired a remarkable reach in recent decades. Sovereign nations now readily submit their domestic policies—or what they once would have considered their domestic policies—to international agreements and supranational institutions. The Kyoto Protocol, for example, seeks to reduce the danger of global warming at the end of the next century by, in effect, rationing energy use among dozens of advanced industrial countries in the present decade. Meanwhile, human rights conventions purport to regulate details of family life and basic operations of labor markets. Those who admire such measures speak of "global governance" and "the end of the nation-state." Those who fear such measures speak of "threats to sovereignty."

For people who think of themselves as practical and hard-headed, it is tempting to dismiss the alarmists as well as the enthusiasts. Both seem to attribute great force to international law, while hard-headed people tend to regard international law as a pious delusion. Yet such hard-headed views are, in their own way, rather naive.

For one thing, a dismissive view of international law is unrealistic as a matter of domestic politics. A very sizable constituency for ambitious international programs already exists within the United States. The Clinton administration and virtually all environmental advocacy groups in America back the Kyoto Protocol. And that venture in international regulation is only the latest in a string of similar international projects, all of which have ardent and influential sponsors in Washington. Dismissive mutterings against international law will hardly derail those sponsors' ambitions.

The second big problem with the "hard-headed" view is that, as an approach to foreign policy, it is dangerously indiscriminate. International law is by no means entirely worthless for the United States. The United States has always sought to maintain some kinds of international agreement and to assure them something like the force of law. It remains true today, as it was in the eighteenth century, that the United States has a very real stake in international agreement regarding rights of passage on the high seas and in international waterways. It remains true today, as it was in the eighteenth century, that the United States has a substantial stake in agreements on trading rights. When we undertake to allow imports to enter the United States with few restrictions, we insist, under international agreements, that other countries provide comparable access for American exports. On the whole, other countries do, in fact, comply with such traditional and practical agreements, so that American compliance brings a substantial and quite tangible return.

The question, then, cannot be whether the United States should support or respect international law in general. The question is whether the United States can accept anything at all that flies under the banner of international law. Those who warn that international law threatens American sovereignty do have one simple but powerful argument on their side. When we let international agreements determine our own policies, we cannot choose different policies for ourselves from those that come to be embraced by "the international community." To that extent, policymaking by international agreement must restrict our own system of self-government at home.

There is a deeper point, however, that shrill warnings about the threat to our democracy from international authority are apt to obscure. The truth is that the United States will not be bound by any international agreements or international controls to which our own government does not consent. But it is also true that our government does not consent to international commitments in the same way that it makes decisions about domestic policy.

The Constitution imposes a whole series of checks and balances on domestic lawmaking. Over the past fifty years, we have also built up a whole series of parallel checks on policymaking by domestic administrative agencies. Under current practice, the U.S. government makes international legal commitments with almost none of those checks. But international commitments are still open to influence from the most attentive and concerned pressure groups. Policy is not really made in secret. It is simply not made through constitutional and accountable procedures.

That sort of extraconstitutional policymaking invites quite unhappy policy outcomes. The risk is that policy will come to reflect not just the priorities or preferences of foreign governments, but also the unscreened nostrums of ardent ideologues and adroit interest groups in our own country. One way or another, we must expect quite distorted results if we allow too much of our own national policy to flow into our system through new international channels, bypassing the traditional channels of constitutional governance in this country.

This book, then, is an argument for reviving the traditional American view on the proper role of international commitments. The Framers of the U.S. Constitution were certainly not disdainful of international law: they provided that treaties be included in the "supreme law of the land" (in Article VI) and gave Congress the power to remedy "offenses against the law of nations" (in Article I, Sec. 8). But the Framers assumed that there were limits on what matters treaty could govern and what questions the law of nations—that is, international law—could settle. Well into the twentieth century, Supreme Court justices and distinguished jurists alluded to such constitutional limitations as self-evident features of our constitutional scheme. Yet earlier generations, operating in a world where international law was far more narrowly confined (by prevailing international practice), saw no need to pin down the precise limits implicit in the American Constitution. This book seeks to clarify what those limits are and to highlight their current relevance.

The effort to delineate such limits seems particularly urgent now because, in the absence of any clear understandings on the matter, we seem to be letting international agreements and international authorities determine more and more of our policy. For various reasons—some of them quite appropriate—courts have generally left it to Congress and the president to decide when American policy can be delegated to international forums or pursued through international agreements. It is up to Congress to establish some limits. That task requires some understanding of the underlying stakes.

A debate on this issue seems quite timely now for another reason. In the 1920s, disputes about American participation in the League of Nations prompted a far-ranging debate about the proper scope of international commitments. After the horrors and upheavals of the Second World War, American leaders in both political parties sought to avoid similar disputes when the United States took its place in the United Nations. In the 1950s, there was another intense debate about U.S. participation in UN human rights agreements and other new international undertakings. But, again, leaders in both parties sought to sideline that debate in the interests of an active American leadership in the cold war.

The end of the cold war has encouraged many people to see a more ambitious role for international law, but it also leaves the United States with the luxury of taking a sober second look at the questions we tried to suppress in more perilous times. The world we face today is, in fact, more like the world of the Framers than the world we faced for most of the twentieth century. No aggressive, looming military power threatens the world in quite the way that Nazi Germany, Imperial Japan, or Soviet Russia did for so many decades. There is no longer any mobilization of the world into rival power blocks, as there was through much of the cold war. In such a world it is possible to retake our bearings by the constitutional principles of safer and saner times.

There is a third reason that a new look at international commitments seems particularly timely at this moment. One of the central problems with international commitments is that they tend to transfer decisionmaking power away from more visible and accountable forums into the hands of foreign policy specialists in the executive branch. That is the latest development in a long-developing pattern. Power has flowed to administrators and executive officials in the federal government for much of the twentieth century. Quite apart from the pressures of world war and cold war, that steady accretion of centralized power was for many decades regarded as the only way to accomplish necessary schemes of national regulation. But hard experience and a great deal of serious scholarship in economics and political science have in the past three decades fostered a renewed respect for the flexibility of markets and the virtues of decentralized decisionmaking. At the same time, legal scholars—and more and more judges—have acquired renewed respect for traditional constitutional forms as barriers against impulsive or factional schemes of control. Federalism, separation of powers, and property rights—central concerns in the constitutional thought of earlier times— have experienced a revival in court reports and in leading law reviews.

International regulation is a detour around those developments. That is precisely its appeal to some of its champions. For others, that may be strong reason to reconsider the current drift to policymaking by international agreements or international institutions. If we wish to revive limitations on government at home, we must revive in this generation the limitations that were assumed by earlier generations to limit governmental commitments abroad.

1

Getting beyond Slogans: Why There Must Be Constitutional Safeguards

Is American sovereignty imperiled? Warnings that it is stir the blood of some Americans and leave others blinking in bewilderment. The end of the cold war has left many people feeling much more optimistic about international cooperation. Others see new international commitments as particularly questionable when the United States no longer faces serious security threats. Some advocates urge that "globalization of trade" requires international standards for protection of workers, consumers, and the environment. Others insist that if such an ambitious agenda must follow in the wake of global trade, America should rethink its commitment to open trade.

On every side there have been earnest appeals to protect American sovereignty. On the left, Ralph Nader and the Sierra Club insist that free trade agreements threaten the sovereign authority of the United States to establish its own regulatory standards—but then support international agreements for environmental protection. At the other end of the spectrum, Pat Buchanan denounces trade agreements as a threat to American sovereignty. Other conservatives, while dismissing that threat, have warned that the Chemical Weapons Convention threatens American sovereignty by opening U.S. chemical plants to international inspection.[1] While advocates on all sides denounce threats to sovereignty, they seem to interpret the term in inconsistent ways and rarely bother to spell out what they actually mean by the term.[2]

If one tries to set aside sloganeering and polemical rhetoric, the underlying principle may seem inherently ambiguous. Sovereignty denotes independence. A sovereign state is one that acknowledges no superior power over its own government—or, as the Declaration of Independence put it, with proper piety, no superior "among the powers of the Earth." But one of the basic attributes of sovereign or independent states is the power to conduct foreign policy and undertake treaty commitments: among the "Acts and Things which Independent States may of right do," the Declaration lists the power to "contract Alliances" and to "establish Commerce." And the U.S. Constitution stipulates that treaties, along with federal statutes, are "the supreme law of the land."

Independent or sovereign nations do sometimes break their treaty commitments. And for well over a century, the Supreme Court has affirmed that treaties have no greater authority than other sources of federal law, at least as far as U.S. courts are concerned.[3] If Congress chooses to enact a statute that contravenes some provision in an existing treaty, that statute and not the treaty will be enforced as "supreme law" within the United States. Just as a later statute takes priority over an earlier statute, so a later statute will, by this understanding, take priority over an earlier treaty.

But that hardly settles the issue. An international commitment remains a commitment and often would serve no purpose if it were not understood as, in some sense, a binding obligation. When American prisoners were massacred by their German captors during World War II, the United States was outraged at that violation of German commitments under international conventions on the treatment of prisoners of war. American indignation was in no way tempered by the reflection that we, ourselves, always had the theoretical option of violating that convention, as a matter of U.S. law.[4] When we enter a trade agreement today, we insist that other countries live up to the terms of the agreement. We do not say to other countries: "Of course, nothing in American law can compel us to adhere to this agreement if we want to violate it, so we assume you will also feel free to violate the agreement whenever you please."

Then too, the notion that we can back out of treaty commitments does not say anything about the kind of commitments we can make in the first place. If it is reassuring that a treaty can always be trumped by a later congressional enactment, advocates can invoke that assurance as license to enter any and all agreements. After all, we can always back out of our commitment if it causes trouble later on, can't we?

Suppose, then, that the United States agreed with Canada and Mexico to strengthen and extend the reach of the North American Free Trade Agreement (NAFTA). Suppose we agreed, under a new treaty, to empower a NAFTA directorate to issue binding standards and directives that could be directly enforced in American courts, in litigation by private parties, without any further action by the U.S. Congress. Suppose that, to ensure that U.S. courts (and the courts of our partners) interpret those rulings properly, the treaty established a new NAFTA high court in Montreal, from which appeals could be pursued by private parties. Suppose that the treaty even empowered that supranational high court to nullify acts of Congress along with enactments of American state legislatures (and their counterparts in other countries) whenever such laws violated terms of the treaty—or the implementing directives of the directorate.

None of those arrangements is unthinkable. Countries in Western Europe have already undertaken all of this under the treaties establishing the European Union.[5] If the United States committed itself to such arrangements, would we still say that the United States was as sovereign as before, because Congress still retained the ultimate power to force withdrawal from the treaty? Government officials in Europe freely concede that the European Union represents a "pooling of sovereignty"—so that no member state is entirely sovereign on its own. Is there no limit on the extent to which the United States can follow the same course?

As it is, the current version of NAFTA allows private litigants to challenge certain U.S. trade measures before a supranational panel, the decisions of which cannot be reviewed but must still be enforced by U.S. domestic courts.[6] In NAFTA side accords, the United States has also agreed that internal regulatory policies on labor conditions and environmental protection—policies aimed at the actions of American citizens on American soil—may be subject to challenge before special NAFTA commissions. Are those aberrant slips? Or are they the first steps on a slippery slope? The European experience suggests that the slope can carry a country on a long descent from full sovereignty—and that sizable constituencies are ready to push for further and faster slides down that slope.

The European Union

The European Union began only forty years ago as the Common Market, with a focus on reducing trade barriers. By the 1980s, the original aims had expanded to the point where the European Commission was imposing complex requirements on a whole array of social policies—to ensure, for example, that women, within each country, receive pay comparable to that of men for jobs of "comparable worth."[7] The expansion is hardly surprising. The reduction of trade barriers necessarily brought new competitive pressures on industries in various member states. Most of the original members—which are still the core powers in the EU—had already built up elaborate structures of state protection for major industries, often in response to (or in conjunction with) pressures from socialist or labor constituencies. Expanding social protections at the European level was a means of compensating or converting potential opponents of economic integration.

In fact, business constituencies have also clamored for wider systems of European regulation—even while supporting free trade in other respects—for free trade necessarily puts special pressures on firms operating in states with high taxes or heavy regulatory burdens. Harmonizing regulatory standards and sharing fiscal burdens across national boundaries are ways of protecting such firms against the competitive advantages of firms operating in states that would otherwise have lower regulatory and tax burdens. So, for example, Germany, which has the most ambitious environmental regulations, has pressed hard in the past two decades—and with much success—to see its own environmental standards imposed on its EU trade partners through EU institutions.[8] In much the same way, a number of German standards for protection of workers have been imposed on Germany's EU partners as the price for gaining access to German markets.[9]

The various trends come together in the case filings before the European Court of Justice. The country most often sued in the past decade has been Germany—mostly by foreign firms seeking readier access to German markets. But Britain, which is one of the EU nations least often charged with maintaining improper import barriers, is nonetheless hauled before the ECJ more often than any other country for failure to comply with EU social policy standards. Those suits are sometimes brought by the career officials of the European Commission, but also quite often by local activists, seeking broader benefits than afforded under British law.[10] And the ECJ demands that Britain adhere to European standards, as developed by the European Commission. So the price of free trade in the European Union has been submission to common regulatory standards, even when those standards have nothing to do with the character of the actual goods traded among

5

EU members. What is now being "traded" in that trade organization is not just goods and services, but differing national preferences on regulatory standards within each country.

The United States is still quite far from committing itself to anything as ambitious as the supranational institutions of the European Union. But the United States has already taken a first step, with the NAFTA side accords, in entangling trade agreements with internal policies on labor and the environment. Both labor leaders and environmentalists have urged that international free trade be tied to more ambitious international standards in those areas. Indeed, when the World Trade Organization was inaugurated in 1995, President Clinton urged that the new organization give immediate attention to drafting an international labor code and integrating new labor and environmental standards into its trade norms.[11]

Observers differ on the degree to which the existing structures of international trade can actually accommodate such initiatives. But certainly the net effect of such measures (if successfully implemented) would be to suppress the choices that individual nations might otherwise make for themselves regarding proper levels of environmental protection and labor market controls. In Europe, economic integration, for all its side ventures in social regulation, does seem on balance to have enlarged markets and fostered economic growth. But it is not easy to say whether business elites support further integration as a means of enlarging markets or as a device for softening competition through Europeanwide controls.

What is beyond dispute is that business leaders do focus on the institutions of the European Union as major centers of policymaking. Accordingly, Brussels, the headquarters of the European Commission and its associated bureaucracies, has now become the lobbying center of Europe. As such, it more than rivals national capitals as a focus of advocacy and deal making by specialized advocates in business and in other sectors.

U.S. Parallels

Our own experience with federal regulation offers an instructive parallel. Before the political upheavals wrought by the New Deal in the 1930s, established constitutional doctrine sought to limit the reach of federal power to matters of genuinely national concern. The Supreme Court interpreted the Commerce Clause of the Constitution (which grants Congress power to regulate "commerce . . . among the states") as applying only to commercial activities crossing state lines, so the federal government was barred from regulating production within the borders of any state. Abandoning that doctrine opened the way for federal regulation on an ever larger scale. And along the way, the politics of regulation changed quite markedly. Whatever other arguments might be raised against new federal regulatory ventures, arguments regarding "states' rights" or constitutional limits on federal power (at least in relation to federalism) almost disappeared from public debate. Knowing that federal regulation was always a possibility, business lobbyists—and lobbyists of every other kind— wasted little time on such principled arguments against new federal initiatives. Instead, they maneuvered to see that any ensuing legislation would, in its details, be more favorable for their own specialized interests.

In time, business lobbies became quite adept at tracking and influencing federal regulatory policies and began to develop a considerable stake in the process. Among other things, business lobbies often sought federal rules that would preempt a patchwork of differing (and sometimes more ambitious) state regulatory policies. So business interests, which might have seemed a natural bulwark against centralized policy, became its ally.

Meanwhile, by the 1960s and 1970s, a growing array of nonbusiness advocacy groups had descended on Washington to clamor for new regulatory benefits or new federal funding provisions or the joining of funding to new regulatory restrictions—for racial minorities and cultural

or language minorities, for feminists and those with handi-
caps, for defenders of the environment and champions of
the consumer. Once constitutional limits on federal authority had eroded, everyone seemed to have a new agenda for
exercising federal power.

By the early 1990s, Congress thought nothing of enacting a law stipulating the volume of water to be used in
flush toilets throughout the United States.[12] The notion that
some matters are properly reserved for states and localities
to determine for themselves—a doctrine that had once fig-
ured quite centrally in the pattern of American politics—
seemed almost to have disappeared from political culture
as well as constitutional law.

Constitutional Boundaries

Signs of a resurgence in older doctrines of federalism have
appeared in the past decade. Supreme Court rulings and
congressional enactments both reflect a new readiness to
curb the reach of federal power. The trend has promise
and may prove increasingly important. But with so many
interests already holding a stake in the existing federal be-
hemoth, that trend faces very great resistance.

In the meantime, the federalization of so much policy
has undoubtedly increased the total volume and cost of
government regulation and introduced new rigidities in
public policy. For most Americans, however, the effect is by
no means unbearable. Thus, it seems plausible to many
people that having moved so much public policy from the
states to the federal government, we can now extend the
pattern, moving more and more policy from the federal to
the international level.

Should we be comfortable, though, in gambling that
a parallel trend at the international level will be equally
tolerable? After all, the states have been declining in social
significance for generations now, as people move frequently
to new jobs in other states, acquiring new friends, new rela-

tives, and even second homes in different states. We are not remotely in that situation with regard to national boundaries. Nor does anyone seriously imagine that a world government could provide a meaningful system of democratic accountability to replace federal authority, as the federal government has provided in displacing the states.

We are still, of course, a very long way from seeing international controls swamp federal politics, in the way that federal authority has preempted state authority within the United States. We have good reasons for thinking that this will never happen. But the point is not the scale of the effect but the pattern. Some people will always favor more extended international controls—at least in some contexts, on some issues. There will always be opponents, too. With no constitutional boundaries, the tendency of political decisionmakers may often be to reach some compromise, resisting the full program of the "internationalists" while discounting the fears of "nationalists" and trying to offer some consolation to both. Over time, the result is not just a gradual accretion of new commitments. The more disturbing result is a shift in the strategic calculations of interest groups and political constituencies: knowing that new international commitments may well come to pass in any case, those groups will focus their energies on influencing policy details rather than try to hold the line of principle that might otherwise halt such policies at the outset.

The function of a constitution is to give force to such lines of principle. Sovereignty might be viewed as one set of lines laid down by the Constitution. In fact, national sovereignty is the presupposition for all the other lines of principle established by the Constitution. Constitutionalism is about legal boundaries. Because the United States is fully sovereign, it can determine for itself what its Constitution will require. And the Constitution necessarily requires that sovereignty be safeguarded so that the Constitution itself can be secure.

2

Constitutional Integrity: The Core of Sovereignty

When the United States declared its independence, it acknowledged that "a decent respect to the opinions of mankind" obliged it to "declare the causes" for that action. It did not, however, wait for international comment on that unilateral statement of its "causes," much less seek international permission for American independence. In its own understanding the United States became an independent nation by its own declaration and its willingness to defend it by force of arms. When the new Constitution was adopted a dozen years later, it grounded its authority solely on that of a sovereign people: "We the people of the United States . . . do ordain and establish this Constitution."[1]

The Constitution limits the powers of government. That is, in the American understanding, one of the main purposes of a constitution. At the same time, the Constitution establishes a division of powers within the government and the forms and procedures through which those powers will be exercised. As the Supreme Court has emphasized in recent decades, even a duly enacted statute cannot transform the basic constitutional scheme; that can only be done by a formal amendment, adopted through the amending procedures laid down in the Constitution itself. Thus, for example, Congress cannot transfer executive powers to officials who are appointed and removed by Congress itself: the separation of powers remains, as the Supreme Court has affirmed, an unavoidable element of the constitutional plan, even if Congress and the president think it convenient to evade that requirement in a particular statutory program. [2] Constitutional requirements must prevail over calculations of administrative or political expediency.

If the Constitution must prevail over federal statutes, must it not also prevail over treaties? Certainly, much authority exists for thinking so. At the outset of our constitutional history, Alexander Hamilton put the point this way:

> The only constitution[al] exception to the power of making treaties is, that it shall not change the Constitution; which results from this fundamental maxim, that a delegated authority cannot alter the constituting act, unless so expressly authorized by the constituting power. An agent cannot new model his own commission. A treaty, for example, cannot transfer the legislative power to the executive department.[3]

Viewed in that light, questions about sovereignty might seem reducible to the question of whether the Constitution authorizes a particular policy—quite apart from its connection with an international treaty. But the matter is not quite so simple. The Supreme Court has repeatedly affirmed that the president has broader powers in foreign affairs than in purely domestic matters.[4] The Court has also held that matters that might otherwise be reserved to state governments can be proper subjects of federal legislation when Congress is legislating to implement treaty commitments.[5] In some respects, then, the exigencies of foreign affairs are thought to justify a relaxation of the constitutional limitations that obtain in domestic affairs. Extending that reasoning, one might be tempted to think that anything at all might be a valid international commitment, if negotiated by the president and duly ratified by the Senate.

An evident logic to such reasoning exists. To take the extreme case, what if the United States were forced to make terrible concessions after defeat in war? Could the Supreme Court repudiate particular elements of the resulting peace treaty on the ground that they violated the Constitution? Would we be forced to return to war rather than suffer an impairment of the Constitution? Or would not the Constitution be adequate to this extreme eventuality, by authorizing the president and the Senate to bind the country on any terms necessary to save American lives? In such an extremity, would not the Constitution allow some of its provisions to be sacrificed by treaty to preserve the rest?

Constitutional Limits on the Treaty Power

Plausible as such reasoning might seem, Supreme Court decisions and the most eminent commentators have generally insisted upon the opposite view—that the Constitution does indeed place unyielding limits on the treaty power. On that view, the Constitution presumes American sovereignty: if the United States were forced to make unconstitutional concessions to buy peace from a relentless enemy, it might still call itself the United States, but it could no longer claim the authority of its original Constitution. The Supreme Court put it this way in 1890:

> The treaty power, as expressed in the Constitution, is in terms unlimited except by those restraints which are found in that instrument against the action of the government or its departments, and those arising from the nature of the government and of that of the States. It would not be contended that it extends so far as to authorize what the Constitution forbids, or a change in the character of the government or in that of one of the States or a cession of any portion of the territory of the latter without its consent. [6]

There have been very few cases in which the Supreme Court has had the occasion to clarify the general terms of that formula. The Court did hold in its 1957 ruling in *Reid v. Covert,* however, that the Constitution's due process guarantees must override international agreements providing for the trial of American civilians by military court martial (even if the civilians are dependents of American military personnel, stationed overseas).[7] The emphatic language of the Court's opinion in *Reid* is worth quoting at length:

> The United States is entirely a creature of the Constitution. Its power and authority have no other source. It can only act in accordance with all the limitations imposed by the Constitution. . . . The concept that the Bill of Rights and other constitutional protections against arbitrary government are inoperative when they become inconvenient or when expediency dictates otherwise is a very dangerous doctrine and if allowed to flourish would destroy the benefit of a written Constitution and undermine the basis of our Government. If our foreign commitments become of such nature that the Government can no longer satisfactorily operate within the bounds laid down by the Constitution, that instrument can be amended by the method which it prescribes.[8]

The decision in *Reid* was also quite emphatic in rejecting the notion that, merely because Article VI of the Constitution includes treaties as part of the "supreme law of the land," treaties are exempt from constitutional limitations:

> [N]o agreement with a foreign nation can confer power on the Congress, or on any other branch of Government, which is free from the restraints of the Constitution. . . . It would be manifestly contrary to the objectives of those who created the Constitution, as well as those who were responsible for the Bill of Rights—let alone alien to our entire constitutional history and tradition—to construe Article VI as permitting the United States to exercise power un-

der an international agreement without observing constitutional prohibitions. In effect, such construction would
permit amendment of that document in a manner not sanc-
tioned by Article V [the provision for amendments]. The
prohibitions of the Constitution were designed to apply to
all branches of the National Government and they cannot
be nullified by the Executive or by the Executive and the
Senate combined. . . . It would be completely anomalous
to say that a treaty need not comply with the Constitution
when such an agreement can be overridden by a statute
that must conform to that instrument.[9]

While the actual decision in *Reid v. Covert* emphasized
restrictions in the Bill of Rights, the Court has observed in
other contexts that the arrangement of powers within the
national government remains a key provision of the constitutional scheme, as much so as the Bill of Rights.[10] Thus, if
treaties cannot override guarantees of civil liberty in the
Bill of Rights, neither, it would seem, can they override fundamental structural principles of the Constitution. From
the earliest period, statesmen and commentators have indeed drawn the inference that treaties would be invalid if
they did not conform to particular power arrangements or-
dained by the Constitution.

So, to take the clearest example, even today most commentators agree that the United States cannot, by treaty,
transfer war powers from Congress to the president.[11] The
United States can certainly promise allies to come to their
defense in the event of war, as we have done, for example,
in the NATO treaty. But the prevailing view today is that
the president could not rely on the treaty—nor on a UN
Security Council resolution—to commit the country to war:
he would have to implement our international commitments by seeking congressional approval for war.

There is, in the same way, near universal agreement
that treaties cannot preempt the congressional power of
the purse. A treaty may commit the United States to pay

money—as, for example, in dues payments to international organizations like the United Nations. But no money can be drawn from the Treasury without a separate appropriation by Congress.[12]

It has long been argued, in a similar spirit, that legislative powers—or treaty-making powers—cannot be delegated by treaty.[13] The argument is that treaties can establish binding law, but only insofar as the treaty itself does so. Thus, the Senate Foreign Relations Committee protested in 1911: "To vest in an outside commission the power to say finally what the treaty means by its very general and indefinite language is to vest in that commission the power to make for us an entirely different treaty from that which we supposed ourselves to be making."[14] Of course, an international body established by treaty might make recommendations. But to make them binding on the United States would require separate and subsequent U.S. action.

Thus, in negotiations leading up to the establishment of the International Labour Organization following the First World War, the United States accepted a role for the ILO in developing labor standards on specific topics. But the United States insisted that each new standard would have to be separately approved by ILO member states in a separate convention and could not bind any state not specifically approving that particular convention.[15] In practice, while the United States has been a participant in the ILO since the 1930s, it has committed itself to hardly any of those specific labor practice conventions.[16] Similarly, when the Reagan administration declined to subscribe to the UN's Law of the Sea Treaty, it emphasized—among other objections—the impropriety of the treaty provision delegating rulemaking and licensing powers to the "Authority," an international agency that would regulate access to mining on the ocean floors. The objection was that, in ratifying the treaty, the United States would not simply commit itself to limitations in the text of the treaty, but also empower that

"Authority" to develop limitations considerably beyond those that the Senate considered and ratified in the original treaty text.[17]

The Analogy with Domestic Practice

The argument against such delegations proceeds from analogy with domestic practice. The Supreme Court has long held that the Constitution sets limits on the extent to which Congress can delegate lawmaking authority, because Congress must be responsible for underlying legislative policy. And the Court has held that delegation to private bodies is "delegation in its most obnoxious form."[18] Can it really be true that the Constitution limits delegation of governmental power to private citizens of the United States but places no limits on delegation to supranational bodies—that is, to foreigners, with even less accountability to the U.S. public?[19] The Constitution vests power where it does, and it is not up to the constitutionally designated organs to reallocate their powers at will.[20]

The same sort of reasoning would apply to the executive. The president has the constitutional duty to "take care that the laws be faithfully executed." That includes the power to see that international treaty obligations are faithfully executed. The grant of power is exclusive: it must be the president (or a subordinate executive officer, constitutionally accountable to the president) who sees to the execution of American treaty obligations—not an international authority. In domestic affairs, Congress cannot superimpose a new chief executive on the constitutional chief executive. It cannot even force the president to implement the determinations of a separate administrative authority.[21] By the same reasoning, the president's authority as commander-in-chief cannot be delegated, even by a treaty negotiated by the president. The president does not have the constitutional authority to yield up his own constitutional responsibilities to an international force.[22]

Finally, it was once well accepted that American courts could not be subject to international appeal. The Constitution vests "the judicial power" in life-tenured judges, appointed by the president and confirmed by the Senate. And "judicial power" has always been understood to mean the power to decide a case with finality, so that courts have refused to rule on hypothetical cases or cases subject to subsequent administrative review. As decisions of "the judicial power" cannot be overruled in a particular case by legislative or executive officials, so they cannot (according to the traditional view) be subject to overruling by foreign courts.[23]

The point is a crucial one. The European Court of Justice operates precisely by such appeals (or "referrals") from national courts, which accept the hierarchical authority of the ECJ by treaty stipulation. The Inter-American Convention on Human Rights establishes a Human Rights Court in San José, Costa Rica, operating on the same system of appeals from national courts.[24] The United States has not ratified the treaty and so does not now permit such appeals. The Carter administration did urge ratification, however, and many human rights advocates in this country have urged that we do change our policy to participate.

In the summer of 1998, a UN conference in Rome produced a plan for a permanent "International Criminal Court," with broad jurisdiction over war crimes and crimes against humanity. The Clinton administration refused to support the plan in its ultimate form for fear that it might expose U.S. military personnel to international prosecutions, when such prosecutions were opposed by the U.S. government. But the administration was prepared to endorse the project if it did allow for a U.S. veto of particular prosecutions. Allowing an international tribunal to review (or supersede) actions by U.S. courts in cases against U.S. citizens was not regarded as a constitutional impropriety in itself, although previous generations would clearly have seen fundamental constitutional objections to such an arrangement.[25]

Meanwhile, the U.S.-Canada Free Trade Agreement and its successor, NAFTA, already provide for appeals by private parties from U.S. administrative proceedings to supranational tribunals. Some scholars have pointed out the constitutional difficulties in this scheme,[26] but it did not raise any great controversy. Legal scholars no longer take the constitutional strictures of earlier times so seriously.

Diminished Accountability

Yet the underlying issue is not simply a matter of observing proper forms. The federal Constitution vests power in federal organs so that the federal government itself bears responsibility—and accountability—for its policies. The internal version of that principle has recently received emphatic affirmation from the Supreme Court in cases dealing with the proper form of federal-state relations. In its 1992 ruling in *New York v. United States*,[27] the Supreme Court insisted that while Congress could enact its own standards on the disposal of radioactive wastes, it could not force states to enact those standards. Though the text of the Constitution is not explicit on this point, the requirement that the federal government enact its own policies through its own organs was held to be implicit in the Constitution's underlying structure:

> [W]here the Federal Government compels States to regulate, the accountability of both state and federal officials is diminished. . . .
>
> [When the] Federal Government . . . makes the decision in full view of the public . . . it will be federal officials that suffer the consequences if the decision turns out to be detrimental or unpopular. But where the Federal Government directs the States to regulate, it may be state officials who will bear the brunt of public disapproval, while the federal officials who devised the regulatory program may remain insulated from the electoral ramifications of their decision. Accountability is thus diminished when, due to

federal coercion, elected state officials cannot regulate in accordance with the views of the local electorate in matters not preempted by federal regulation.[28]

The Court made a similar point in its 1997 ruling in *Printz v. United States,*[29] where it struck down a federal law requiring state and local law enforcement officials to run checks on gun purchasers under a federal gun control program. Allowing Congress to commandeer state and local officials to implement a federal program would not only undermine electoral accountability, the Court noted, but would derange the Constitution's arrangements of power at the federal level. If Congress can delegate enforcement of its own policies to state officials, it can contrive to have implementation of federal law escape from the required accountability of federal officials to the president, while also evading the accountability implicit in the federal budget process.

If the Constitution does not allow Congress to shift the burdens or responsibilities of federal programs onto the states, can the Constitution really permit Congress to do the same thing by delegating special powers to international agencies? All the same problems of diminished accountability arise in international delegations as in delegations to the states. In some ways, the accountability problem is exacerbated, because state officials do have continuing accountability to American voters while international authorities do not.

The problem here cannot be escaped by invoking the special character of international commitments. International commitments do, of course, involve other countries. But a treaty (or other international commitment) is still a federal policy, binding for the United States precisely because U.S. authorities have said that it is. Our own government, which makes the commitment, must retain responsibility for the way the commitment is implemented. Otherwise, the treaty power would be a way to short-circuit the entire constitutional scheme. We would start with a system

19

that has powers carefully limited and balanced, with continuing structures of accountability, and find that, by international delegations, we end up with policy being made and implemented by outside powers, operating entirely apart from our own constitutional structure of accountability. Surely, that cannot be consistent with the Constitution.

The Constitution may not be explicit in limiting delegations to international authorities. But those limits are, after all, at least as apparent, from the logic and structure of the Constitution, as the limits that the Court has found on delegations to the states. And it is more understandable, in the case of international delegations, why the Framers did not express the prohibition more directly. The contemporary arrangements that challenge the prohibition—such as international agencies, empowered to issue binding regulations or decide private disputes—were unknown at the time the Constitution was drafted and scarcely even dreamed of.

Where the Constitution's Framers did know about an international practice that seemed to jeopardize national sovereignty, however, they took care to control it directly. In Article I, Sec. 9, the Constitution prohibits Congress from conferring titles of nobility and then immediately goes on to prohibit any official who holds an "Office of Profit or Trust" under the United States from accepting any "Emolument, Office, or Title, of any kind whatever, from any King, Prince, or foreign State." Even in the eighteenth century, some people thought it noble to look beyond their own borders and receive recognition for their larger aims and wider contributions. The Framers took care to make that illegal, at least for those in the public service of the American people.[30] American citizens can work for international agencies. But they cannot work for the U.S. government when they serve an international agency. And international agencies cannot do the work of the U.S. government—not in the precise sense of formulating, implementing, or adjudicating the legal obligations of U.S. citizens or the U.S. government.

The Need for Further Limits

Such procedural or institutional brakes cannot be the sole safeguard of sovereignty, however. If treaties mean anything, a promise to do something remains a promise that has strong preemptive claims on American policymakers. If the government can make such promises on any subject and under any and all circumstances, it can insulate a vast range of policies from the free determination of the American political system. What has already been promised to other countries, after all, cannot be readily or freely reconsidered, even if new elections demonstrate that most Americans would prefer a different course.

It is not sufficient, then, to ensure that American treaty commitments are only implemented by constitutional organs of the United States. The initial policy reflected in the treaty is often a sizable policy commitment in itself, regardless of how the details are subsequently handled. And the normal constitutional method for making American policy commitments is to secure agreement of the House, the Senate, and the president—not the president, Senate, and a foreign government or a hundred foreign governments acting through an international body. Constitutional integrity thus implies that there are limits on what can be taken out of the normal constitutional process for making laws and transferred to international negotiations by the treaty power.

Here, too, there is a long tradition of asserting such limits. As far back as the eighteenth century, authorities insisted that the treaty power could be deployed only for proper objects of international action.[31] In the nineteenth century, when the Supreme Court affirmed that treaties could not alter the form of our government, it also insisted that the subject matter of treaties be limited to matters "properly the subject of negotiation with a foreign country."[32] In 1929 Chief Justice Hughes of the U.S. Supreme Court—who had already served as a justice on the Permanent Court of International Justice—reaffirmed the doctrine that the treaty power cannot be invoked as a mere pretext for altering domestic policies: "[T]he treaty-making power is intended for the purpose of having treaties made relating to foreign affairs and not to make laws for the people of the United States in their internal concerns through the exercise of the asserted treaty-making power."[33] As late as the 1960s, that doctrine was still affirmed in the Second *Restatement on Foreign Relations Law*.[34] Though the restatements are compiled by private scholars and do not have the force of law, they have considerable prestige and authority as accounts of what is (ostensibly) already settled law.

Chapter 6 will return to those limitations on the subject matter of treaties. For the present, the point to notice is that earlier generations took the existence of such limitations for granted. Today, leading scholars do not simply ignore but actually deny those limitations. So, by the mid-1980s, the Third *Restatement* expressly repudiated the notion that the treaty power extends only to proper subjects of international negotiation. Instead, it maintained that no distinction between properly international and properly domestic matters could any longer be discerned.[35] So, in the view of leading scholars, anything might be the proper subject of a treaty.

That view became plausible as scholars began to think of international law as having limitless reach—or, at least, as having a reach whose limits could not be specified. The treaty power came to be viewed in a new light as it was reconceived to deal with a far more ambitious conception of international law. But the new conception of international law is quite troubling in itself.

3

The Expanding Reach of International Law: From the "Law of Nations" to "Global Governance"

kepticism of international law is an old tradition in the United States. The expression "globaloney"—a staple of current polemics—had already been deployed in congressional debate in 1943.[1] A generation earlier, the Senate refused to endorse American participation in the League of Nations, unless certain safeguards of American sovereignty were first stipulated (and the Covenant of the League could not be ratified when such stipulations, opposed by President Wilson, failed to gain the necessary two-thirds support in the Senate).[2] Even at the Constitutional Convention in 1787, delegates cautioned against placing excessive confidence in an independent law of nations.[3]

The Law of Nations

Yet there is also a long American tradition of respect for international law. Thus, even under the Articles of Confederation, Congress enacted legislation acknowledging American obligations under the law of nations as a way of asserting the full participation of the United States in the ranks of independent nations. When the new Constitution was drafted, it included among the powers of Congress the power to define and punish offenses against the "law of nations."[4] Shortly after the Constitution was ratified and the new government organized, Supreme Court Justice James Wilson, who had been a leading participant at the Philadelphia convention, gave a series of public lectures on American law that began with an extended admonition on the importance of honoring the law of nations.[5] James Madison, often called the "father" of the Constitution, thought it worthwhile to publish a pamphlet on the law of nations when he served as secretary of state under President Jefferson.[6]

The Founding generation was respectful of international law—or the law of nations, as it was then called— because it conceived of that law as making quite different claims from those now associated with international law. It is worth looking at each of the distinctive features of the original understanding to see why, taken together, the law of nations did not seem to pose any real threat to sovereignty in the view of earlier generations of American statesmen.

First, the law of nations was much more limited in its subject matter or focus than what is now called international law. Much of what was called the law of nations was concerned with sorting out matters of jurisdiction—to decide, for example, when courts of one nation could invoke jurisdiction over a national of another country, or over a contract signed in another country, or over property owned by a national of another country, without affronting the government of that other country. American courts (and their counterparts in other countries) now treat most of those issues under technical doctrines, sometimes called private international law. There was also a large, developed body of law concerning rights of seizure on the high seas in time of war, covering, for example, the claims brought by owners of merchant ships or of cargoes seized by naval forces enforcing blockades. Britain and other European countries had for centuries maintained special prize courts to adjudicate such claims. The United States immediately copied their example, and American prize courts began to apply and extend what they took to be the established precedents.

Second, the law of nations had not only a limited reach but a limited range. As that law was largely about war and commerce—and particularly the interaction of naval war with seagoing cargo—it was largely the concern of the great naval and commercial powers. Most of the relevant precedents came from a handful of great commercial and seagoing powers, with court rulings from Britain, France, and Holland carrying the most weight by the eighteenth century. Well into the nineteenth century, it was common for treatises to speak of the law of nations as a law applying only to "civilized nations" or "Christian nations," which were thought to share common legal traditions in this area.[7] Certainly, it was a law shaped by countries engaged in continuing commercial exchange and repeated, if intermittent, conflict, so that all had some incentive to observe reciprocal restraints.

Third, the law of nations was almost entirely dependent on reciprocal restraints, for it was a law developed in the absence of international institutions, let alone organized international enforcement. Essentially, the law of nations was a law applied by the national courts of the participating countries. No permanent international court existed until the twentieth century. It was considered a remarkable novelty when, in the Jay Treaty of 1794, the United States and Great Britain agreed to submit their conflicting claims (regarding property seizures during the American Revolutionary War) to a special commission of jurists organized for the purpose. Though such ad hoc arbitration commissions would become more common in the nineteenth century, they remained exceptional. Essentially, the law of nations was gleaned, at the time of the American Founding and for generations thereafter, from "the decisions of those tribunals to whom, in every country, the administration of that branch of jurisprudence is specially intrusted," as James Kent's *Commentaries on American Law* put it in 1826, in the first American treatise to give extended attention to the subject.[8]

Particularly notable is that, while Kent does acknowledge that the "opinions of eminent statesmen and writings of distinguished jurists" are worthy of "great consideration" in settling disputed points, his treatment of the law of nations makes no mention of treaties. When Henry Wheaton published the first full-length American treatise on international law a decade later—by which time, the new term *international law* was coming to replace *the law of nations*—he did mention treaties but disparaged their significance: no one treaty could determine the content of international law, since treaties might be broken. Only a long string of treaties embracing the same point could securely establish a disputed point on the meaning of international law.[9]

The traditional view also disparaged treaties for a different reason. It sought to connect historic practice with a version of natural law. It would, as Kent put it, "be improper to separate this law entirely from natural jurisprudence and not consider it as deriving much of its force and dignity from the . . . law of nature."[10] It was supposed then that the law of nations had a logic and authority transcending the stipulations of treaties, so that a treaty could, in fact, be described as contrary to the law of nations.

A last point about the law of nations, in the traditional understanding, follows from the others: the law of nations took the sovereignty of nations as its basic premise. The relevant "law of nature" was the law that applies in a "state of nature" where there is no common judge and each individual is free to do as he likes, if he does not violate the rights of others. Relations among nations were seen as governed, ultimately, by that law of nature because sovereign nations, acknowledging no higher authority, remained in a state of nature with respect to each other.

That reasoning is spelled out in *Le Droit des Gens* (*The Law of Nations*), the mid–eighteenth century treatise by the Swiss diplomat Emmerich de Vattel, which was the leading text on the subject at the time of the American Founding and indeed the text most frequently cited by the American Founders.[11] Vattel was quite emphatic about the principle of national sovereignty: "Of all the rights possessed by a nation, that of sovereignty is doubtless the most important." Accordingly, "[n]o foreign state may inquire into the manner in which a sovereign [prince] rules, nor set itself up as a judge of his [internal] conduct nor force him to make changes in his administration. . . . [I]t is for the nation [over which he rules] to take action."[12] Kent's *Commentaries* takes the same view:

> [E]ach nation has a right to govern itself as it may think proper and no nation is entitled to dictate a form of government or religion or a course of internal policy to another. No state is entitled to take cognizance or notice of the domestic administration of another state or what passes within it as between the government and its own subjects.[13]

Treaties did not, then, change the traditional understanding of sovereignty. It was not thought that they could change it: "If the interference [in the affairs of a sovereign state by an outside power] is itself unlawful [under the law of nations], can any previously existing stipulation make it lawful?" The question was raised by W. H. Halleck's treatise on the eve of the Civil War—and then answered in these confident terms: "We think not; for the reason that a contract against public morals has no binding force and there is more merit in its breach than in its fulfillment."[14] Not the U.S. Constitution nor some other domestic law, but the fundamental doctrine in the law of nations itself would condemn a treaty that interfered with national sovereignty.[15] Similar arguments were repeated by distinguished European jurists and still given a respectful hearing by English texts in the early twentieth century.[16]

International Law in the Twentieth Century

Such views have been largely forgotten in the course of the twentieth century, however. The change in international law parallels wider and better known trends in domestic law. Natural law and natural rights were no longer in philosophic fashion by the end of the nineteenth century. The change in philosophy encouraged (or at any rate mirrored) larger political trends, as the individualist doctrines of the eighteenth and nineteenth centuries gave way to increasingly collectivist visions. As legal theorists questioned the meaning or priority of property rights in domestic law, so others found it easier to question the meaning or authority of national sovereignty—traditionally understood, after all, as a sort of communal property right to the national territory. Similarly, the growth of statute law, at the expense of common law traditions, encouraged legal positivism. Law came to be seen as the will of the dominant power in the community—and needing no more justification or authority. In the twentieth century, a growing tendency in international law was to associate "the law" with the stipulations of treaties. And the number and reach of treaties dramatically increased.

By the early part of the twentieth century, the world could, in fact, look back on impressive achievements in international cooperation. Privateering—the practice of authorizing buccaneering attacks on the commerce of belligerents as a tactic of war—ceased from the Mediterranean and the Atlantic in the mid-nineteenth century, and the legal change could be dated quite precisely to the Treaty of Paris in 1856, whereby the European powers agreed among themselves to forswear that practice. Where the law of nations had long accepted "privateering," it was rendered "contrary to international law" in one successful treaty negotiation.[17] In the following decades, international "unions" were established to coordinate postal deliveries, telegraphic connections, and various maritime practices, and all proved quite successful.[18]

What such examples showed was that international law did not always have to depend on long-established "customary" practice. It could sometimes be coaxed into new provisions with energetic diplomacy. The twentieth century has accordingly seen vast increases in the number of treaties, including multilateral conventions that some scholars began to describe as "legislative treaties."[19] At the same time, the twentieth century has witnessed increasingly ambitious ventures associated with such treaties. On the eve of the First World War, major European states were discussing a multilateral treaty to standardize conditions of labor. The Covenant of the League of Nations, along with its better-known provisions on the preservation of peace, also included specific provisions to encourage international cooperation on labor, narcotics control, and other social matters. The International Labour Organization, sponsored by the League, proved to be one of its enduring legacies. When the United Nations was organized in 1945 as successor to the League of Nations, it gave itself a still wider mandate—reaching into human rights, economic and social welfare, and other matters.

For all the changed expectations of international law, however, it is far from clear that the world itself has changed quite so much. In the era of the American Founding, Alexander Hamilton had confidently asserted that "legislation for communities as contradistinguished from individuals, as it is a solecism in theory, so in practice it is subversive of the ends of civil polity."[20] What he meant was that a government must have full governing power, that Americans could not expect the benefits of a federal government, limiting and superseding the governments of the states, unless the federal government had power to act as a real government, enforcing its authority directly on individual citizens rather than operating through the states.

Much of the argument in *The Federalist* is an extended exposition on the difference between international agreements and actual governing structures. The Articles of Confederation, after all, presented the original thirteen states as binding themselves only to a "firm league of friendship," within which each state would still retain its "sovereignty, freedom and independence." The Confederation government was given the power to establish courts to adjudicate disputes between the states, but no power to enforce the legal consequences of such decisions as they might affect the rights of citizens within those states. The Articles of Confederation did not even give the government the power to raise its own revenue or to field its own army, leaving it simply to requisition the state governments for supply.

The Federalist insisted that such an arrangement, in trying to have it both ways, was bound to fail. Either the federal government must retain ultimate governing authority—drawing its share of the "interests" and "attachments" that follow in the wake of real, governing power—or Americans must be prepared to see the confederation break down and the states go their separate ways. Under far less favorable circumstances, however, contemporary international law tries to do what the Founders regarded as impossible. In the most fundamental respects, it tries to have it both ways.

The Charter of the United Nations gives seemingly wide jurisdiction to that organization but not much effectual power. Over its five-decade history, the UN has continually expanded its jurisdiction while failing to augment its actual coercive power. The point is not that the UN has failed to stop war. Criminal laws do not stop all crime, either. Nor, to follow the analogy with the American experience, did the existence of a federal constitution prevent eleven southern states from organizing a rebellion in 1860. But the U.S. Constitution did make it possible for the federal government to mobilize adequate resources to suppress the rebellion—even at the cost of a terrible civil war. By contrast, the UN Charter is designed to prevent a world mobilization.

The UN Charter purports to give the Security Council the authority to order sanctions, even against nonmember states that threaten the peace (and to order all the member states to cooperate in the resulting sanctions). But the charter also gives each one of the five great powers (as they were in 1945) the authority to veto any Security Council resolution with which it disagrees—on whatever grounds. So the countries in the best position to sponsor aggression are guaranteed the authority to nullify any UN action against that aggression. Even when the UN has called for boycotts, it has failed to mobilize sufficient authority to enforce such boycotts against cheaters.

While it has been largely irrelevant to cold war, regional war, or even horrifying episodes of mass murder, the UN has busied itself proclaiming high ideals. One of its first great ventures, completed with much fanfare in 1948, was the Convention on the Prevention and Punishment of the Crime of Genocide. By the early 1970s, most countries—including Cambodia, Yugoslavia, and Rwanda—had duly ratified the convention. The UN has since moved on to champion endangered flora and fauna—as well as the sexual equality of women, the moral autonomy of children, and the cultural rights of indigenous peoples.[21]

Although the charter specifies (Art. 2, ¶ 7) that none of its provisions "shall authorize the United Nations to intervene in matters which are essentially within the domestic jurisdiction of any state," nothing has ever been found so "essentially domestic" as to exclude UN intrusions. Some scholars assert that the charter's exclusion of "essentially domestic" issues does not apply, in any case, when the UN's actions are not binding.[22] Yet it is not clear that this category ("nonbinding") identifies a distinctive subset of UN actions.

At the least, countries vary considerably in their readiness to be bound by international authority. The fact should hardly be surprising. Countries vary quite widely in their respect for law—or their notions of what the rule of law requires—within their own domestic systems. A "law" does not have the same meaning in China as it does in Canada, nor in the United States of Brazil as in the United States of America—nor even in Italy as in Britain.[23]

It may be true, as prominent scholars have asserted, that most countries obey international law most of the time.[24] It is also true that most gangsters obey most law most of the time, as they have no incentive or no occasion to violate a vast amount of law—from land-use zoning requirements to auto safety inspections. It remains true that, compared with the maritime law of the eighteenth century, contemporary international regulation seeks to coordinate a vastly enlarged range of countries and cultures over a vastly extended range of activities. Yet the "society of nations" is not evidently more of a civil society—answering to a common law from a common authority—than it was then.

The Rise of "Soft Law"

Symptomatic of the problem—and of the eagerness of international agreements to evade it—is the rise in the past two decades of a whole new category of international law: what international law commentators now call "soft law." Particularly in international environmental regulation, but also in human rights and other fields, international conferences now frequently emerge with declarations, frameworks, or statements of principle rather than formal treaties. In effect, such documents are affirmations of good intentions rather than commitments to act in a particular way. They seek to alter the atmosphere of international affairs rather than the actual conduct of states. Soft law is often made through nonbinding declarations or resolutions of the UN General Assembly, and it bears approximately the same relation to law (as traditionally conceived) as the General Assembly does to a legislature.

Such soft law, as a French commentator has noted, seems to escape traditional categories "because it is either not yet or not only law."[25] The hope is that soft law can be eased into practice and then hardened, either in subsequent treaties or by acceptance as customary international law. (See chapter 5.) For those who believe in the process, then, the proliferation of soft law agreements is a hopeful sign. The existence of the category may reflect an actual absence of agreement among states—or an unwillingness to commit themselves—but displays of good intentions hold hope, in such a view, for better things in the future. And some observers are very hopeful, indeed.

Thus, the Commission on Global Governance, charged with recommending reforms in the UN system, admonished the world only recently that "national boundaries are . . . less relevant," and "in certain fields sovereignty has to be exercised collectively"— that is, through international institutions—and sometimes "the fundamental interests of humanity [must] . . . prevail over the ordinary rights of particular states."[26] Among other things, the commission recommends that the great powers agree to phase out the use of their veto power on the Security Council, that the UN develop a parliamentary forum of elected representatives for "the peoples," and that an economic security council be developed to coordinate world trade and foster consumption reductions in affluent countries and wealth transfers to poor countries. The commission also urges action on an extended agenda for reform of international policies on trade, the environment, human rights, labor standards, and many other fields. When terms like *global governance* are used with such confidence, it is fair to question whether the ambitions of international law have not become quite disconnected from its actual capacities.

4

The Real Threats from
"Global Governance"

I f sovereignty is defined as the *ultimate* authority to reject outside control, then all talk of threats to American sovereignty may appear quite absurd, especially
while America remains the world's only superpower. But
that is, as we have seen, an extremely crude way of viewing
the question of sovereignty.

The real threat is not that the United States will be
forced to act against the determined resolve of the American political system. Rather, the threat is that international
commitments will distort or derange the normal workings
of our own system, leaving it less able to resolve policy disputes in ways acceptable to the American people. Global
governance, then, does not threaten to replace the American government, but it does threaten to distract and con-
fuse and, ultimately, to weaken it.

In the short run, the threat is that international commitments will be used to manipulate policy outcomes within
the United States. In the longer run, that trend is likely to
generate some disturbing reactions—some of which may
undermine legitimate foreign policy concerns, as impulsive rejections of particular international commitments
make it harder to maintain other, more serious commitments. In the still longer run, global governance may breed

a dangerous degree of cynicism or sheer paranoia about our own system of government.

The potential for distorting U.S. policymaking is almost inherent in the nature of international commitments. Treaties are bargains among governments. Almost by definition, then, a treaty will impose some compromises on what most Americans might otherwise prefer.

Of course, there are circumstances in which reciprocally binding commitments can be quite useful to foreign policy—which is why the U.S. Constitution does include an explicit process for binding the United States by formal treaty. But the constitutionally prescribed process is deliberately onerous, requiring an unusual two-thirds majority in the Senate to ratify a treaty. Even so, the traditional view was that only treaties on proper subjects and with a constitutionally proper form would be valid.

Evading Checks and Balances

As the traditional limits on the treaty power have been forgotten, ways have been found to circumvent the cumbersome constitutional procedure for making treaties. Executive-legislative agreements—requiring approval by simple majorities in the House and Senate rather than the difficult two-thirds majority—have been adopted in place of treaties for major international commitments, notably the trade agreements.[1] Trade agreements are now usually negotiated under a fast-track authorization, by which Congress agrees in advance to accept or reject the agreement as a whole, without attempting to impose specific reservations or limiting "understandings," as the Senate has traditionally done in treaty ratification. Even when international agreements are cast as treaties, moreover, they are often devised as frameworks for an evolving policy that subsequent protocols will clarify. The original treaty may be submitted for Senate ratification while the subsequent protocols are approved by executive agreement, requiring only presidential signature (without subsequent Senate ratification).

There are, at present, no generally accepted limits on what an executive agreement can accomplish. Even in the nineteenth century, Congress authorized presidents to negotiate standardized postal exchange and tariff reduction agreements. The Supreme Court endorsed the practice in the early part of the twentieth century, in a decision recognizing that executive agreements in such circumstances have the force of law.[2] Before the Second World War, the Court also recognized that the president has certain inherent powers that allow him, incident to recognizing a foreign government, to make executive agreements that even without congressional authorization or ratification may still have the force of law within the United States.[3] The president's inherent powers as commander-in-chief have also been thought to allow him to make certain military agreements on his own authority. But whatever the ultimate limits on the president's authority to make executive agreements, it cannot be said that his authority has been used sparingly—at least not in recent times. In the first hundred years after the adoption of the Constitution, the United States ratified 277 treaties, and presidents made 265 executive agreements. Over the next century, the number of treaties had tripled, while the number of executive agreements multiplied more than twenty-five-fold. Between 1980 and 1992, another 4,510 executive agreements were concluded and only 218 further treaties.[4] Congress has required presidents to provide notification of new agreements but has set down no other limitations.[5]

Even if the initial policy commitment is made by treaty, however, the process is quite different from the ordinary legislative process. New legislation requires reconciled majorities in both the House and the Senate, followed by approval from the president. And those successive agreements (House, Senate, president) must occur in the same session of Congress or else the bill must start from scratch in the next session (where newly elected members may have different views or previous supporters of the bill may have changed their own views). International commitments are negotiated by the executive and submitted for congressional or Senate approval only afterwards (if then). The requirement of contemporaneous consent does not apply. A treaty can wait for years until a favorable majority develops. Many agreements, moreover, are simply left as executive agreements, without ever being submitted for Senate ratification or congressional review.

When it comes to international policy, then, the normal constitutional system of checks and balances is severely reduced. As one prominent scholar of international law has put it, "international commitments" pose "an important problem today" that "arises from the tendency of internationalization to shift powers and responsibilities from national and subnational units with active, reachable legislative bodies to remote international bureaucracies."[6]

Even in domestic affairs, it is true, Congress has allowed much policy initiative to shift to executive agencies. Modern legislation often sketches a broad outline and leaves administrative agencies to fill in the details. So it may seem, for example, that the Environmental Protection Agency sets the terms of environmental policy almost as much as the House and the Senate. It is sometimes argued, therefore, that we can learn to accommodate expanded treaty commitments and international institutions, as we have learned to accommodate powerful administrative agencies.[7]

But the broad powers of administrative agencies have been a source of concern since the 1930s. And they are still a source of concern to many observers. The concern is not only that the absence of checks and balances leads to more regulation than Congress itself would approve but that open-ended delegation encourages the domination of policy by specialized interest groups, capturing or disproportionately influencing an isolated agency in ways they could not do with Congress as a whole.[8] There are now signs that courts have begun to share that concern and may, in a proper case, still enforce some version of the nondele-gation doctrine.[9]

In the meantime, however, policymakers have made considerable efforts to develop checks on administrative authority in domestic affairs. Administrative agencies are subject to procedural constraints on their rulemaking, li-censing, and adjudicatory powers under the Administra-tive Procedure Act or their own organic statutes. Apart from requirements of public notice and due process, agencies must act without arbitrariness and in conformity with their statutory authority. Domestic agencies must hold open meetings and are required to release documents and data under the Freedom of Information Act. All these require-ments can be enforced by appeal to the courts. None of those requirements, however, applies to international agen-cies, nor are their actions subject to judicial review. Inter-national agencies are not required to observe any proce-dures, let alone procedures that appellate courts can force them to respect.

In the American system, moreover, federal adminis-trative agencies must worry about annual appropriation reviews and the threat of budget disciplines. International agencies and programs are not dependent on congressional appropriations (at any rate, not exclusively so), nor are they subject to regular congressional oversight. Proposals have been advanced to develop more transparency and open process in international programs.[10] But those proposals are not likely to go very far, since most countries do not share the U.S. commitment to open government and for-mal process.

The Politics of International Regulation

Is the participation of so many different governments an assurance of caution and constraint—a sort of international counterpart to the competition of interests that tempers congressional decisionmaking? The diversity of national interests is a genuine check on international undertakings in some settings. But it is not something to be relied upon in all fields of international regulation.

To begin with, bargaining over the precise terms of international agreements is not usually a free-for-all with hundreds of distinct players. The member states of the European Union will usually agree in advance on a common European position, which carries great weight because it represents such a sizable portion of the developed world. Less-developed countries often follow the lead of a few larger countries, like India and China. Negotiations, moreover, tend to be left to a large extent in the hands of specialized representatives, so that trade officials negotiate trade agreements, environmental specialists negotiate environmental agreements, and social welfare specialists negotiate human rights agreements. Over the past decade, political scientists have emphasized the way in which such specialized international negotiations tend to generate common assumptions and attitudes among the specialized participants—"epistemic communities" of officials who see the world in the same ways.[11]

Other factors, too, have smoothed national jealousies and bridged national differences in a heterogeneous world, allowing international regulatory projects to gain new momentum over the past two decades. One is that new kinds of international agreements sometimes can tap into larger hopes with much broader appeal. Each new agreement can be touted as a symbol of international cooperation, as a symbol of international concern—and perhaps as a symbol of progress on rather different agendas. European countries, for example, have long sought to ensure that their own system of extensive welfare-state provisions will be extended to their competitors and so have strongly supported international standards that incorporate such measures as imperative "human rights." Less-developed countries have readily signed such ambitious conventions, on the understanding that they will not really be held to any substantial level of compliance. Some of the most brutal governments in the world have cheerfully subscribed to international human rights guarantees; some of the most wretchedly poor states have solemnly pledged to provide educational, medical, and family services, when they cannot even organize themselves to ensure food distribution in periods of famine.[12]

Meanwhile, less-developed countries have for more than two decades sought to use the United Nations to advance their demands for massive wealth transfers from the rich nations of the "North" to the poor countries of the "South." What made it possible to reach international agreement on control of chlorofluorocarbons (CFCs) at the end of the 1980s was that the developed countries promised to provide financial assistance to less-developed countries to help finance their transition to new refrigerants that were judged less threatening to the ozone layer in the atmosphere.[13] In the event, the scale of assistance was far less than needed to cover the costs of that transition—but among less-developed countries, the level of compliance with new norms was also far from perfect. And if, as some critics warned, the less-developed countries suffer some serious public health problems from the loss of affordable refrigerants, the governments of such countries tend to be less vulnerable to democratic pressures from their own peoples, anyway.[14]

In a similar way, less-developed countries agreed to the Basel Convention on trade in toxic substances, which prohibits developed countries from shipping listed materials to outside countries.[15] In effect, the European Union constructed a reprocessing cartel, requiring that recycling of materials be restricted largely to Europe, where the German government was particularly keen to route business into favored, local reprocessing facilities.[16] Less-developed countries found that venture in international control appealing because, whatever its drawbacks, it remained a symbol of Western concern about environmental problems in the less-developed world.

NGO Activism

Another factor that gives special momentum to international control ventures is the increasing role of nongovernmental organizations (NGOs). The media skills of organizations like Greenpeace have helped to build generalized constituencies for those ventures in leading Western countries. At the same time, such organizations have become important players in the negotiations, sending their own specialists to monitor and often to lobby governmental negotiators at each successive gathering in a series of rolling negotiations. Greenpeace and other international environmental advocacy groups have been particularly adept at building alliances with less-developed countries. So, at the urging of Western environmental groups, less-developed countries signed onto a Convention on International Trade in Endangered Species.[17] CITES may actually thwart realistic conservation efforts in poor countries, insofar as it eliminates economic incentives for local people to protect potentially valuable wildlife. It has, however, helped Western environmental advocates, the most enthusiastic champions of CITES, to pose as special defenders of the elephant and the panda.[18]

Sensing the political value of nongovernmental advocates (at least in certain controlled settings), the United Nations Environment Program has offered them a visible platform at international gatherings. Western governments have also been particularly accommodating to such organizations, providing facilities and background briefings and helping them to link up with counterpart groups from other countries and to advance positions with delegations of other countries.[19] The 1992 UN Earth Summit in Rio was, by design, as much a summit for environmental advocacy groups as for governments. According to the Commission on Global Governance:

> In the interlinked global conferences that have followed the Rio meeting, NGOs continued to have a strong impact on both the preparatory processes and the conferences.

... More and more, NGOs are helping to set public policy agendas—identifying and defining critical issues, and providing policymakers with advice and assistance. It is this movement beyond advocacy and the provision of services towards broader participation in the public policy realm that has such significance for governance.[20]

If one steps back from the details, one can discern the outline of a political arena that is an international projection of the style of public-interest advocacy politics that developed in the United States in the 1970s. Some of the same groups that have been most active in American advocacy politics have become most active in counterpart forums at the international level and describe their involvement in similar terms.[21] Such groups have gained new allies in European governments and governments of less-developed countries, pursuing their own agendas for their own reasons. They have gained new prestige or new pathos by globalizing their rhetoric, shifting from endangered locales in the United States to "our endangered planet." The groups transfer deliberation from U.S. forums, where opposing interests know how to mobilize opposition, to strange new forums in distant capitals, where internationally oriented advocacy groups have a comparative advantage. More important, the groups transfer deliberations from the U.S. political system, with its own set of checks and balances, to international gatherings with none of those safeguards. The active, informal lobbying by activist NGOs, especially when international conference organizers encourage it, cannot replace the system of formal, procedural controls under which U.S. agencies operate.

Internationalist Momentum

In some countries, hesitant governments have clearly used international agreements to build domestic support for controversial policies favored by particular constituencies.[22] In the United States, it must be said, international commitments have moved forward without much scrutiny or check at home, because their effects have still been rather peripheral. A few important checks remain in place. If a treaty has to be ratified, that can still be a severe hurdle. The Senate has not yet ratified the Basel Convention, for example. More tellingly, despite much mobilizing of support by feminist organizations and a wide array of liberal advocacy groups, the Senate has refused to consider ratification of either the UN's Convention on the Elimination of All Forms of Discrimination against Women (1980) or the UN's subsequent Convention on the Rights of the Child (1989). Those treaties bestow the status of "human rights" (and "international obligation") on an array of feminist or liberal policy preferences, from comparable-worth regulation of the economy—to ensure that women are paid equally for job performance of "comparable worth"—to government-sponsored child care for working mothers to special protection for children from receiving instruction or reading matter disfavored by their parents.[23]

But the potential remains for more substantial influence down the road. Even a skeptical Republican Senate felt obliged to ratify the Chemical Weapons Convention in 1997, despite the fact that its value was largely eviscerated from the outset by the nonparticipation of those countries—most notably, Iraq, Iran, Russia, China, and Libya—most likely to use such weapons in the future. Environmental agreements also seem to carry great momentum. Even the skeptical Bush administration felt compelled, in the election year of 1992, to sign a Framework Convention on Climate Change at the Earth Summit in Rio de Janeiro. The Senate was then readily persuaded to ratify that down payment on a program to forestall a much-disputed threat of global warming.

While the Bush administration did not support the Biodiversity Treaty developed at the Earth Summit, the Clinton administration subsequently did sign the treaty. The United States has, accordingly, participated in the drafting of a subsidiary Biodiversity Protocol with other signatories to the main treaty—even though the Senate has not yet ratified the Biodiversity Treaty. This episode illustrates another factor that gives extra momentum to international agreements. As noted at the outset of this chapter, unsuccessful bills in Congress die at the end of the session, but treaties can be readily revived in the Senate, years after their initial negotiation. And while the treaty is still pending before the Senate, a determined administration can proceed to further negotiations and implementing plans, as if the treaty were already ratified.

Meanwhile, the Senate often does go along with questionable international ventures because, as in the case of the Framework Convention on Climate Change, the initial commitment seems largely a matter of symbolism. At the outset, many international commitments often are little more than that. Such treaties lack hard or fast commitments with accompanying international enforcement mechanisms. But initial commitments may turn into much more ambitious ventures down the road—as has happened with the international commitment to control global warming. In the meantime, a general treaty commitment may give rhetorical leverage to domestic advocacy groups. Having made the initial commitment and participated in continuing negotiations for more detailed or substantive commitments, the United States then faces pressures—not least from domestic advocacy groups—to make good on its commitment.

In fact, subsequent measures are not always subject to Senate ratification. For example, the Senate did ratify the Montreal Protocol, promising a gradual, long-term phaseout of products emitting CFCs. When subsequent rounds of negotiation resolved to make the phaseout much faster and more thorough (in the London and Copenhagen Protocols), the EPA was empowered to implement those more ambitious standards under the Clean Air Act, after the president (on his own) agreed to them.

True, the U.S. Congress can always defy any commitment—even one ratified by the Senate—with countering legislation. That fact does not justify complacency, however, and is in some degree an actual cause for concern. It is irresponsible to embark on open-ended commitments, with no clear limits on how far we might go, while trusting that we can, if need be, always break our word later on. That is rather like speeding off in a car that is known to have faulty steering, because we are confident that we can always slam on the brakes if the car comes to a sharp curve. We should not be so sure that the brakes will hold if there is no limit on our acceleration beforehand. We should be rather anxious, too, about the price of sudden, sharp brakings.

One problem here is that we often do depend on other countries to honor their own commitments. When we negotiate an agreement to eliminate CFC production, we expect other countries to do likewise—which, in fact, all Western countries have now done. If the United States is seen to break its commitments capriciously and impulsively, other countries become more reluctant to take their obligations seriously or even to negotiate in full seriousness. That is already a problem and can become a much more serious problem.

As it is, Americans are quick to protest when trade agreements yield a result that seems unfavorable to American interests. Politicians are quick to denounce agreements or interpretations of agreements as one-sided. That problem is perfectly familiar in domestic policy, where critics often protest that regulatory schemes impose unequal burdens with questionable or unequal benefits. But Americans feel some obligation to American domestic law, even where it seems questionable or unreasonable in its requirements, because it is still our own law. We put up with the law because we are bound to put up with each other. That is what makes us one country—that we put up with irksome burdens rather than risk descending into anarchy or extreme division.

Until recent decades, international law did not pretend to make ambitious claims on the generality of nations. It traditionally recognized that the "community of nations" is not, after all, much of a community. An ambitious international law was seen as an invitation to lawlessness. International law used to be founded on respect for sovereignty, because it understood that all law, in some sense, must be founded on sovereignty—on the authority of actual communities, with the capacity to mobilize and direct force in continuing, predictable ways.

The Danger of Backlash

Setting overly high goals for international law is bound to promote cynicism—when it does no worse. It can do worse when commitments that were not expected to mean much of anything turn out to have some bite after all. Then, setting high goals risks provoking angry, frustrated outbursts that sweep aside reasonable, long-standing international understandings along with the new and questionable. It is too soon to know how the most ambitious commitments, like the proposed Kyoto Protocol on global warming, will play out. But we have already had a foretaste of the syndrome on a smaller scale.

Back in 1972, the Nixon administration persuaded the Senate to ratify U.S. adherence to the World Heritage Convention, a seemingly innocuous treaty under which countries proposed historic or scenic sites for the international equivalent of a landmarks registry.[24] In 1995 the U.S. government invited the UN's World Heritage Committee (charged under the convention with monitoring the safekeeping of "world heritage sites") to offer its views about a proposed mining operation some two miles outside the boundary of Yellowstone National Park, one of the registered U.S. sites. Without waiting for the completion of a local environmental impact statement, then in preparation by Montana officials, the committee toured the site and issued its own strong statement of disapproval against the mining proposal.

When that intervention provoked a local uproar, Republicans in the House of Representatives responded with a reasonable bill to require specific congressional approval before any sites in the United States could be submitted to international inspection. As the bill moved through the House, however, it was amended to specify, as well, that mining operations on federal lands should be limited to U.S.-owned companies—an entirely unreasonable measure that violates accepted international understandings and risks costly retaliations against American operations in other countries. Such abusive reactions are to be expected when Congress is provoked into impulsive reactions against questionable international obligations.

The other long-term risk is that cynicism and anger come to infect our own domestic law and politics, as new norms pop up from nowhere, inspiring some people with unreasonable hopes and others with wild fears. In the Yellowstone affair, environmental advocacy groups, which opposed mining in the vicinity of the park, were the first to seek international inspection by the World Heritage Committee—as if an international panel could settle a domestic dispute on a matter with no real international ramifications. Local citizens in Montana, Idaho, and Wyoming were initially dumbfounded and then outraged to find that a local dispute about mining operations in their area had somehow been turned into cause for UN intervention. Some of their reactions betrayed a disturbing degree of paranoid concern about the UN—which was supposed to be readying international helicopter patrols to take over the park.[25] Fears about the UN, however, were clearly also fears about the connivance of the U.S. government in an international intrigue.

Such incidents certainly will not plunge the United States into civil war. But they do have the potential to fan the flames of paranoia among people whose suspicions of federal authority are already disturbingly deep. The truth is that, once irate citizens began to ask why the Yellowstone mining dispute was any business of the UN, the U.S. government could not offer any convincing answer. Instead, it denied that recommendations of the UN's World Heritage Committee would determine U.S. policy. But what, then, were officials from Thailand, Germany, and other remote countries doing on an inspection trip to Montana?[26] If the World Heritage Convention is meaningless, why did the United States subscribe to it?

We should not be surprised at such episodes—for all the seeming irrationality in the responses of local citizens and Washington politicians. Something is inherently unsettling and disorienting in the underlying situation. A constitution is supposed to impart some degree of regularity or predictability to the exercise of power. International legislation is a product of an international system that is not, in any meaningful sense, constituted to make "legislation." When policy is made in international forums, there is often a great risk that some people will view the results as absurd—and others as outrageous. From such opening perceptions, cool, calculating responses are not likely to flow.

5

Flowing through the Cracks:
The Perils of Soft Law

Iinternational law has many avenues into the American
political system. Treaties are, of course, the most direct
and traditional path. An exclusive focus on treaties,
however, may prompt one to think that international commitments can be kept in check simply by the vigilance of
the Senate. In fact, many international commitments are
now made by executive agreement, without formal ratification by the Senate. Even with formal treaties, what seems at
the outset a rather innocuous agreement may draw the
United States into a continuing political or regulatory involvement, with unanticipated and sometimes quite startling consequences. All such patterns are matters for concern, as the previous chapter argued. But those patterns
hardly exhaust the concerns Americans ought to have about
the incursion of international law into our own political
system, for treaties, it turns out, are not the only route into
the American legal system.

Human rights treaties are the most notable example
of the problem. Wary of subjecting such a basic element of
American policy to foreign judgments, the Senate long re-
fused to ratify any international human rights conventions.
When the Reagan administration urged ratification of the
Genocide Convention, the Senate gave its consent in 1988,

but only after attaching an extensive series of reservations, understandings, and declarations to its ratification, which seemingly nullified any actual application of the convention to U.S. law.[1] That must have seemed a clever response to a cleverly posed challenge.

The Genocide Convention, after all, is filled with ambiguous provisions, some of which have no connection to murder but might well be invoked in connection with disputed domestic policies.[2] At the same time, the existence of that treaty clearly had no serious value in deterring barbarous regimes from committing mass murder, since regimes capable of such monstrous crime are more than capable of the additional offense of signing an international commitment in bad faith. The treaty appeared to many senators as a disturbingly broad series of policy commitments—or a legal handhold to advocates seeking such commitments—wrapped up in a pious affirmation. Who could oppose a treaty against mass murder? So the Senate met the problem head-on; it piously affirmed the principle and then quietly rejected all its legal implications.

That compromise seemed so convenient that the Senate adopted it, in almost the same terms, when it proceeded to ratify other UN human rights conventions, notably the broad International Covenant on Civil and Political Rights in 1992 and the more specialized conventions against torture and against race discrimination.[3] It would seem from those ratification instruments that the conventions cannot be invoked in U.S. courts. No doubt that is what most senators expected, but they probably did not reckon with the remarkably protean character of contemporary international law.

Customary International Law

Along with treaties, international law has always had an element of uncodified practice, now called "customary international law." As noted in chapter 3, most of international law, in the era of the American Founding, was actually "customary law" in this sense: it was not the product of specific formal agreements but of long-established practice. On the eve of the American Revolution, William Blackstone's famous *Commentaries on the Laws of England* had described the "law of nations" as part of the common law of England.[4] A few decades later, James Kent's *Commentaries on American Law* described that part of the common law as already taken over by American courts, along with so much else in the English common law.[5] As late as 1900, the U.S. Supreme Court, in a case dealing with the seizure of a Spanish fishing vessel, applied customary law principles and justified its ruling with the affirmation that "international law is a part of our law."[6]

All of that should now be of mere historical interest, however. Some issues, like the capture of civilian vessels as "prize" of war that occupied the Supreme Court in 1900, have disappeared from courts, because the practices involved have nearly disappeared in the modern world. Now, formal treaty regulates such traditional subjects as the treatment of ambassadors, and formal U.S. statutes regulate the liability of foreign governments.[7] Since a 1938 decision of the Supreme Court, moreover, federal courts have repudiated any claim to elaborate their own version of common law.[8] When common law norms arise in a federal case (because there is no relevant statutory authority), federal courts are now supposed to apply the common law as received and understood in the state where the case arose—and American state courts have not been active in developing distinctive new theories about the law of nations.

Nonetheless, customary international law has staged a remarkable revival in federal courts. The great breakthrough was the 1980 Court of Appeals decision in *Filartiga v. Pena-Irala.*[9] The suit was brought by Paraguayan citizens (who happened then to be residing in the United States), protesting the murder of a Paraguayan, by a Paraguayan government official, that took place within the borders of

Paraguay. A federal district judge, baffled to find that matter in a U.S. court, had initially dismissed the claim for want
of jurisdiction, but the Court of Appeals for the Second
Circuit reversed. It found jurisdiction under the Alien Tort
Statute enacted in 1789.[10] That statute, dealing with "offenses against the law of nations," had been enacted to ensure federal remedies for wrongs committed against foreign ambassadors during their service in the United States—
since protection of ambassadors was a central tenet of the
law of nations, as understood in 1789. The Second Circuit
Court of Appeals, cheered on by a host of international law
scholars,[11] insisted, however, that "customary international
law" has greatly expanded and now incorporates an international law of human rights. So the case went forward to
an eventual judgment, which included punitive damages
against the defendant (who, back in Paraguay, gave no indication of any willingness to pay anything to anybody on
the mere say-so of a U.S. court).

Harold Koh, a professor at the Yale Law School and a
prominent commentator on international law, has described that ruling as the "*Brown v. Board* . . . [of]
transnational public law litigation."[12] The claim may be
somewhat hyperbolic, but Koh clearly has a point. Like
Brown, the *Filartiga* ruling has indeed spawned a string of
similar (and often similarly "successful") suits, applying the
Filartiga reading of customary international law under the
Alien Tort Statute.[13] Moreover, like *Brown*, the *Filartiga* ruling has served to advance a new view of what litigation is
about—a new view, at least, for private litigation in international law. Cases like *Filartiga* are no longer about providing a remedy to a distinct victim under well-established law.
They can promise little more than moral satisfaction to the
actual victims, since the perpetrators of human rights abuses
in other countries are typically beyond the actual reach of
U.S. courts. Instead, such cases are about advancing a "law
reform" agenda—or perhaps, more accurately, a political
reform agenda—by accumulating moral or rhetorical leverage in successive precedents. The ultimate target is not

the practice of other countries but the policy of the U.S. government.

One can hardly dismiss this trend as an isolated aberration. The Third *Restatement of Foreign Relations Law,* published in the mid-1980s and still the most highly regarded nonofficial survey of U.S. law in this field, devotes an entire separate section to customary human rights law.[14] The previous *Restatement* (published in the mid-1960s) was entirely silent on that subject. In the view of the latest *Restatement,* however, a new and separate "federal common law" exists to deal with distinctive issues of foreign relations. It does not parallel state law but supersedes the law of individual American states. It is a law directly available to federal judges.

Though serious scholars still dispute each of these claims,[15] the *Restatement* purports to be describing legal doctrines that are already settled in American law. The customary international law of human rights is, according to the *Restatement* (and a growing number of precedents), already part of American law. But this human rights law is quite expressly and deliberately conceived as "open-ended."[16] How far might it go?

To start with, it says so much about the free-floating character of "customary international law" (as seen by many commentators) that it was invoked in *Filartiga* to justify a practice that was the opposite of customary. No other country at that time had invoked international human rights norms in its own courts against abuses perpetrated by officials of other countries, who acted against citizens of those other countries and within the borders of those other countries. Indeed, the customary view was that national courts must beware of intruding into the internal affairs of other countries. That may well remain the customary view in much of the world.[17] But changing that aspect of customary law was not the real point.

Perhaps the most notable thing about *Filartiga*—and its subsequent canonization in the *Restatement*—is that it invoked, as evidence of "customary international law," human rights conventions that neither the United States nor Paraguay had ratified. That was not an inadvertent move, nor is it, in the minds of many commentators, a lawyerly dodge. Treaty law establishes a direct obligation to the terms of the treaty. Customary international law is something different—a more generalized obligation arising from accepted practice, for which treaty law is not so much the source as one piece of evidence. Hence, one can argue that the United States still accepts as a matter of customary law that which it has refused to ratify. Indeed, that position has much appeal to our own State Department in other contexts: the Reagan administration, which refused to ratify the UN's Law of the Sea Treaty, nonetheless held that certain of its provisions, regarding rights of passage on the high seas, had become established as "customary international law."[18] Thus, it may seem quite reasonable to regard the various Senate reservations attached to the human rights conventions as having no relevance to the substance of those conventions when viewed as customary international law—which might, in that status, be seen as binding law for the United States, even where the treaties do not, in themselves, have direct force.

Once "customary international law" is seen as binding international law, a series of legal consequences plausibly follows. Of course, that law will take precedence over contrary enactments of American state or local governments, just as any federal law would.[19] Distinguished commentators also argue that since customary law has the same status as a treaty, it must take precedence over earlier federal statutes—just as a later treaty would supersede an earlier statute.[20] Since it is impossible, moreover, to fix with any precision the point at which a doctrine of customary law has been settled for the United States, it would not be difficult to postdate many claims and conceive them as "later in time" to a particular, inconvenient federal statute. Some commentators even claim that, as a part of international law, customary law norms should also be seen as binding on the president and executive agencies—and enforced as such by federal courts.[21]

To appreciate the potential scope of this challenge, we must recall (from chapter 3) some basic elements in the modern transformation of international law. First, where the traditional view saw the law of nations as resting on *long-established* custom (related, in turn, to basic laws of nature), the modern view sees international law as highly malleable, so that new doctrines of "law" can be coaxed into existence in a very brief time.[22] Second, the traditional law of nations was built on respect for sovereignty: it was, in fact, mostly aimed at clarifying lines of demarcation between the otherwise conflicting claims of sovereign states. By contrast, contemporary international law sees nothing as excluded, in principle, from international legal controls. Both those differences come much into play in the field of customary human rights law and tend, in fact, to reinforce each other in extending the potential reach of the relevant "law."

Freed from its traditional moorings, international law no longer needs to be demonstrated by actual practice. Recall that Kent looked to the pronouncements of actual courts in actual cases as evidence of the settled practice of other nations. International human rights law is not the product of court rulings, but of international conferences. Abstract pronouncements are enough. At that, they need not even be the authoritative pronouncements of supreme governmental authorities. Words spoken by diplomats at conferences are given much weight, and then the reconfiguring of those words by commentators is supposed to give more weight, and the repetition of the words by yet other commentators is thought to lend still more weight to contentions about the law. Soon there is a towering edifice of words, which is then treated as a secure marker of "customary international law." The field of human rights is particularly open to that approach, since the relevant UN conventions provide no real enforcement mechanism but simply call for governments to submit reports and respond to criticism.[23] Louis Sohn of the Harvard Law School, one of the principal reporters for the Third *Restatement,* has put the point quite candidly: "[S]tates never really make international law on the subject of human rights. It is made by the people who care: the professors, the writers of textbooks and casebooks, and the authors of leading articles in leading international law journals."[24]

Encroachment of Customary Law on Domestic Policy

All this means that the content of customary law can change quite rapidly simply as the view of scholars may change. Viewed as a law that each country applies or interprets for itself, the law can be whatever some group of "experts" persuades a judge to think it may be. For that reason, it is likely to reach more and more deeply into domestic affairs. If a norm in customary international law exists against race discrimination, why not also against sex discrimination? And then why not also against discrimination on the basis of citizenship or language or sexual orientation? Why not affirm state duties like enforcement of comparable-worth regulation (to ensure that jobs of equal value receive equal pay) or public provision for day-care facilities?[25]

Until now, the process has operated almost exclusively through the Alien Tort Statute and on a rather narrow range of claims about violent abuses in foreign countries.[26] But the doctrine that lower courts have been building in such cases, with the enthusiastic encouragement of scholars, would seem to have much wider reach. If customary international law is a part of our law that U.S. courts can apply in cases involving aliens, why not also in cases involving U.S. citizens in disputes with state and local governments or indeed in disputes against the federal government? The Alien Tort Statute may be a special statute for aliens, but customary international law, as its leading academic expositors see it, is a law of much wider scope.[27]

So far, the Supreme Court has been quite resistant to invoking customary international law as a restraint on the foreign policy prerogatives of the executive, and lower courts have followed that lead.[28] But suppose that the federal executive itself invokes customary international law to bolster a certain position in domestic litigation? The prospect is hardly remote. In *Filartiga*, officials of the State Department—during the Carter administration, which had unsuccessfully urged U.S. ratification of human rights conventions on the Senate—filed papers with the Court of Appeals supporting the invocation of customary international law in that case. And that seems to have been decisive for the outcome. It is not hard to imagine the same thing's being done in other contexts with more dramatic effect on domestic law.

First, there is the question of statutory interpretation. It is a long-standing rule, dating to Chief Justice Marshall in the early nineteenth century, that U.S. statutes should be interpreted to accord with international law whenever that is possible.[29] It would require only a bit of extra ingenuity to claim that various regulatory statutes, particularly those relating to civil rights, should be interpreted more broadly to accord with international human rights standards, binding on the United States as a matter of customary international law.[30] Does the existing federal statute on sex discrimination in employment (Title VII of the 1964 Civil Rights Act) mandate comparable-worth regulation? Federal appeals courts have all said no,[31] but they were not pressed in the 1980s to consider an evolving doctrine of customary international law, which might now require a different view of the statute. Some scholars have already taken the next step and argued that constitutional standards should be reinterpreted to permit the United States to come into accord with international standards.[32]

Seeds of such legal maneuvers have already yielded some sprouts. In the mid-1980s, the Supreme Court made explicit reference to international human rights norms in

57

holding that the execution of someone under the age of sixteen would be improper.[33] The Court did not base its holding on the precise claim that customary international law must be controlling, but only three justices objected to the introduction of such material as an interpretive guide to the Constitution. The Supreme Court in recent years has been somewhat reluctant to take activist leaps beyond the evident meaning of the Constitution. But a Court with a slightly different set of justices, operating in a slightly different political climate, might well be tempted to invoke international law as a safer path to preferred policies.[34]

Consider, for example, the case of *Romer v. Evans*,[35] where the Supreme Court held that Colorado had violated the Equal Protection Clause of the Fourteenth Amendment by adopting a statewide prohibition on gay rights measures. The Court was unwilling to argue that there is a constitutional right to engage in homosexual practices—an argument it had confronted and narrowly rejected in 1987. So the Court instead relied on a rather strained claim about the irrationality of prohibiting only gay rights measures and no others. That argument avoided setting a clear and immovable precedent but still sent a signal that courts would scrutinize antigay bias. For a Court seeking such flexibility, international law might have provided an attractive approach. Suppose that the Justice Department had made this appeal—that the Colorado measure was in conflict with customary international law. The doctrine is already in place for such a move.[36] Once a major Supreme Court decision endorses it, there can be a flood of new applications.

Three considerations make such a trend a serious prospect. The first is that the doctrine has been put in place, not by a few speculative articles, but by a continuous and quite systematic effort by a sizable contingent of legal scholars. The relevant section of the Third *Restatement* is already a powerful vindication for that continuing effort, citing scholars who cite other scholars in what purports to be a restatement of the currently settled "law."[37] Dozens of law journals specifically devoted to international law have sprung up in law schools throughout the United States in just the past two decades.[38] Together with special international law programs (quite a few specifically devoted to international human rights issues), those journals nurture a community of like-minded advocates. If judges are too busy to read the relevant law reviews, those scholars reach out to them by more direct means. The Aspen Institute now offers federal judges special seminars, run by adherents of the broad modern view of customary international law and its application to human rights.[39]

Meanwhile, advocacy groups systematically disseminate the domestic application of human rights norms. The American Civil Liberties Union publishes annual reviews of U.S. human rights practices in cooperation with Human Rights Watch—an organization that, while it devotes most of its attention to human rights abuses abroad, has drawn many of its top figures from the ACLU.[40] And the doctrines of that community now pop up regularly in legal briefs on a range of issues seemingly quite removed from international human rights. Only two years ago, when the Ninth Circuit Court of Appeals reviewed the legal merits of California's Proposition 209 (forbidding racial preferences in state universities and state employment), the court was confronted with a detailed amicus brief, claiming that Proposition 209 was in violation of international human rights norms.[41] Once the Supreme Court gives more direct encouragement, advocacy groups are poised to exploit that opening to the full.

A second point to keep in mind is that while plaintiffs will have well-rehearsed briefs, provided by a well-organized advocacy community, the defense lawyers in such suits—particularly those serving state and local governments—will likely be quite disoriented by arguments from international law, a field quite removed from their own practice. Even if they seek outside help, local authorities will find that contrary views on international law are quite hard to come by.

That is almost certainly so if they seek pro bono assistance from academic experts, because, of those with the time and inclination to take a hand in litigation, the overwhelming majority (to judge from the law reviews and past experience in Alien Tort Statute cases) will favor the other side. Such circumstances will produce great pressure to settle cases without developing all the possible opposing arguments in costly appeals. A few such cases can generate momentum that helps tip the scales in many others. In such a way, a new trend may settle into place, without the Supreme Court's having to commit itself with much authoritative guidance. That was the way in which lower court experiments with prison reform or remedial racial quotas settled into place.

A final point to consider is that arguments from customary international law will likely have special appeal to courts precisely because the relevant law remains so malleable. Customary international law is like a grand buffet from which each jurist may take some particular delicacy and then leave the rest for those with different tastes. International law is not, in fact, a law that all countries truly apply to the same extent. It is a law available to the browser and the enthusiast, a law that invites selective application—in other words, a special kind of law.

That international law will have applications to controversial matters like gay rights is easy to predict. Human rights law is set up in just that way—as a soft law. In 1992 the UN Human Rights Committee found that the Commonwealth of Australia was in violation of the Covenant on Civil and Political Rights because one of its component states (Tasmania) still had a traditional antisodomy law on its books. It is safe to say that, when the covenant was drafted in the 1950s, no one thought its vague and general clauses added up to a gay rights guarantee. It is equally safe to say that most countries represented on the Human Rights Committee (which included a number of regimes with notably repressive policies toward homosexuals[42]) did not regard their decision as establishing a new rule that would be binding on their own countries. The ruling is soft law, which is up to the country concerned to adopt or reject.

It was easy to anticipate, however, that Australia would accept the UN finding: the federal government had conceded in its briefs that the state of Tasmania was in violation of international norms. The federal government was in the hands of a Labor government, which had taken strong public positions in favor of gay rights, while the state government of Tasmania was in the hands of a conservative coalition, which had expressly defended the state's traditional laws on sexual morality in the previous election and still received a local mandate for a new term in office. At the same time, it was convenient for the federal Australian government to consider itself bound by international law in this matter. By invoking "treaty commitments," the federal government gave itself jurisdiction in a policy matter normally reserved to state governments under Australia's federal constitution. But invoking international "obligations" in that matter was also quite safe for the federal government. Shortly after it invoked the Human Rights Committee's ruling to intervene against Tasmania, the federal government of Australia announced that it would not feel bound by international rulings on immigration procedure—a subject where some of its other constituencies were much more resistant to international views.[43] Australia would be bound only where it chose to be bound.

Customary international law can work a similar magic for American officials. A pronouncement from some international conference can be paraded as evidence of the current international standard in some controversial policy matter. It will not be necessary to document that all countries or even most countries actually conform to the standard in practice, let alone to show that two-thirds of the Senate had formally endorsed that standard in a particular treaty. The federal executive (seconded by a small army of international law experts) might then invoke obligations under customary international law to support a particular claim in a lawsuit against a state or local government. Courts might embrace the particular claim on the understanding that the executive is sharing the political heat and that, at any rate, the argument can be rejected on any number of grounds in the next case where international law appears in a less attractive context.

The whole argument rests at bottom on a simple premise. Most commentators agree that a country can exclude itself from an emerging norm in customary international law if the dissenting country expressly opposes the norm in the course of its development. That seeming concession actually makes it much easier to say that a new norm has emerged with universal agreement, except for those countries that reject it. So far as the United States is concerned, the argument suggests that what is not directly repudiated by Congress (or the president) has been tacitly endorsed.[44] In that way, law can be made for the United States in international forums rather than in American legislatures.

Wholesale Delegation

In that sense, customary international law is, in itself, a wholesale delegation of lawmaking power (or treaty-making power) of just the sort that, as we saw in chapter 2, the Constitution would otherwise seem to forbid. True, subsequent congressional action can override that law—if the president does not veto it or if very large majorities favor an override. But the traditional rejection of such wholesale delegations of congressional power is in no way answered by that consideration, which applies just as much, after all, to wholesale delegations to domestic administrative agencies. The underlying problem remains the same: wholesale delegations allow initiative and responsibility to shift from elected officials in a carefully structured process to an amorphous outside power, neither electorally accountable nor constitutionally structured.

Indeed, we have no reason to think that if such a process gains momentum, it will be restricted to a special category of human rights concerns. The most crucial point about the customary international law of human rights is that it is not, as now conceived by commentators, a bounded or special category at all. Thus, some advocates now claim that human rights include a general right to a safe or protected natural environment—a right, after all, that many international treaties seem designed to vindicate. And some federal courts have begun to endorse that view in suits protesting "environmental torts" by U.S. firms operating in other countries.[45] Other commentators see regulations of labor markets and labor relations as a matter of human rights.[46]

Where Americans have tended to think of human rights or basic rights in terms of freedom from government, international human rights law puts at least equal emphasis on claims to government benefits. Thus, along with the Covenant on Civil and Political Rights is a companion Covenant on Economic and Social Rights, which makes no provision for the protection of private property but includes extensive guarantees relating to job security, pensions, and schooling. The United States has not ratified the latter convention, but most of the world has done so, and the United States might plausibly be said to have accepted it—or parts of it—as a matter of customary international law. In the end, U.S. courts can embrace customary law, even without giving it a special rubric as a matter of human rights. Thus, one might say that the United States has tacitly endorsed a whole range of customary norms under different headings, without ratifying the relevant "human rights" conventions.

As the whole process hinges on the silence of Congress, however, it can be readily restrained by a loud and emphatic legislative rejection. Almost all commentators acknowledge that, at least as a matter of U.S. law, Congress retains the power to overrule any norm of customary international law—blocking its application in U.S. courts—whatever the rest of the world may think. Such a measure may soon require urgent attention. If Congress does not take action, we face the serious danger that international law will not simply provide a flow of policy into our own system through discrete channels, which might at least be subject to individualized scrutiny in legislative hearings. Instead, we may awake to find that international law has turned into a free-floating vapor, infiltrating American law through untold cracks and leaks, shaping our own policy to the preferences of people who like people who clink glasses at international gatherings—perfectly nice people, perhaps, but not having any real accountability in the American constitutional scheme.

All the legal premises for such developments are now in place, and no established doctrine exists that would stand in their way. If Congress does not act, it will be simply trusting to good luck—or to the right political mood in federal courts—to prevent customary international law from sprouting into domestic policy, like weeds in an untended garden. If that happens, it might even be reasonable to infer that Congress has tacitly endorsed the emerging trend by not putting a stop to it. As it is, some advocates claim that Congress has tacitly endorsed the current use of the Alien Tort Statute by enacting a companion statute in 1991, the Torture Victim Protection Act, without imposing any limits on continuing resort to the Alien Tort Statute.[47] But we are not supposed to make basic policy by tacit endorsement.

If it makes any sense to acknowledge customary international law as binding, that law ought to be confined to truly international concerns, at least as far as Americans are concerned. To confine customary international law in that way, of course, would require a clear sense of the boundary between properly international and properly domestic concerns. It is difficult to discern such a boundary, after so many decades of scholarly effort to obscure the relevant distinctions. But it would not be impossible to restore such lines, if Congress were determined to do so. And it would be well worth the effort, if we still care about preserving the fundamentals of self-government under our traditional constitutional system.

6

Preserving the Domestic Character
of Domestic Affairs

Some elements of international law can be quite compatible with national sovereignty. That is the reason earlier generations of American statesmen, while hardly indifferent to American sovereignty, were generally quite respectful toward international law. The law of nations, as the Founders understood it, was aimed largely at defining the rights of sovereign nations, so that nations would keep out of each other's internal affairs. Much contemporary international law still has that aim. And many other aims—like reducing barriers to international trade—are also quite traditional and quite compatible with the sovereignty of nations in their own, domestic governance.

The threat to national sovereignty arises in two circumstances: where international legal commitments improperly intrude on the machinery of domestic governance and where they improperly intrude on the substantive content of domestic policy. Regarding the former, we can still insist (as discussed in chapter 2) that all international commitments must be implemented, within the United States, by proper constitutional authorities of our own government. We can insist, in the same spirit, that the United States will be obligated by treaties, but not by subsequent protocols or grand elaborations of those treaties if they are not separately ratified.

Regarding the substantive content of international commitments, it is harder to draw sharp lines. In a world where the UN has been allowed to exercise supervisory authority over sexual mores and local flora, it is tempting to conclude that clear lines no longer exist between properly domestic and properly international affairs. It is so tempting that prominent legal scholars have readily succumbed to the temptation. Thus, as noted in chapter 2, the latest *Restatement of Foreign Relations Law* (1987) has abandoned the doctrine of the previous *Restatement* and openly asserts that the treaty power cannot be limited to "international" concerns (or that such a limitation now has no meaning).

While the *Restatement* purports to be a summary of "settled law," there are good grounds to doubt that such an interpretation has been settled. For one thing, no decisions of the Supreme Court have actually endorsed that open-ended view. A still better reason for doubting that view is that it cannot be true. At least if one accepts that the Constitution does have some fixed and determinate meaning, the treaty power cannot be entirely open-ended as to the content of treaties.

Subject-Matter Limits

For those moved by historical arguments regarding "original meaning," the evidence is overwhelming that the Founders saw the treaty power as limited to proper subjects of international negotiation. When, for example, Patrick Henry charged in the Virginia ratifying convention that the new Constitution would allow federal authorities to "make any treaty . . . as they please," James Madison was emphatic in his response: "The exercise of the power must be consistent with the objects of the delegation. . . . The object of treaties is the regulation of intercourse with foreign nations and is external."[1] Proponents of the new Constitution identified the treaty power with "war, peace and commerce."[2] They therefore assured critics of the new Constitution that treaties would be relatively rare and would never affect the domestic rights of American citizens.[3]

Federalists may have had rhetorical reasons to downplay the reach of the treaty power during the ratification debates. Yet leading figures affirmed substantially the same views even after the Constitution was secured. Madison and others, for example, emphasized the limited scope of the treaty power in the debate over the Jay Treaty in 1796, the first great debate in Congress on the meaning of the treaty power.[4] And later generations seem rarely to have doubted the conclusion. All through the nineteenth century and well into the twentieth century, Supreme Court justices and the most respected commentators held to the same underlying view—that the treaty power authorized commitments only on those matters "properly the subject of negotiation with a foreign country."[5]

Even without such historical evidence, however, it would still be clear that the treaty power cannot be entirely open-ended. The Constitution goes to considerable trouble to enumerate the powers of Congress (and of federal courts), with the evident purpose of confining the reach of federal power. If the treaty power has no limits, then part of the government can always reach, through the back door of the treaty power, what the government as a whole has been so carefully excluded from reaching.

Until recently, that point might have seemed a bit anachronistic. For some decades after the New Deal, it is true, the Supreme Court interpreted the enumerated powers of Congress so broadly that it seemed to place no serious limit on the reach of federal legislation. But in the past decade, the Supreme Court has repeatedly affirmed that the doctrine of enumerated powers does remain a restriction on Congress.[6] In striking down overreaching federal statutes, the Supreme Court has emphasized that limits on congressional power must be enforced to protect the reserved powers of the states. It is hard to conceive that the Constitution imposes limits on federal legislative power to protect the reserved powers of the states but places no limits on the treaty power—which, after all, not only threatens the states (since treaties will override state law) but also threatens the internal governing power of the United States as a whole.[7] Federalism is often (if misleadingly) described as a system that secures the "sovereignty" of the states. It would be incongruous—indeed, altogether bizarre—if the Constitution turned out to protect the sovereignty of the fifty states from federal legislative encroachment but did nothing to protect state sovereignty or even the sovereignty of the federal government itself from encroachments by treaty.[8]

Limits on the Power to Make International Treaties

Many scholars now assume that such structural arguments can be readily trumped by appealing to the complexity and interdependence of today's world. As a practical matter, they say, no easy way exists to distinguish international from domestic affairs. The same argument was long thought to show that there was no longer any possibility of distinguishing properly federal from properly state concerns. But that argument no longer persuades the Supreme Court. Recent decisions have insisted that when Congress purports to exercise its power to regulate "commerce among the states," its enactments must deal with matters that actually do concern commerce and do concern things that move across state lines.[9] By analogous reasoning, one can still discern at least two firm rules limiting the power to make international agreements: they must be genuinely *international* and must be genuine *agreements*. Both requirements are implicit in the traditional accounts of the treaty power, and both follow from the inherent logic of the treaty power.

First, regarding the requirement that a treaty concern matters that are genuinely international, the most obvious and reliable test is whether the treaty concerns something that actually crosses a border.[10] It is easy to conjure with speculative chains of causation, projected through remote connections, to show that a particular event in one country can exert some ultimate if indirect effect on the state of affairs in some other country. By just such reasoning the congressional power to regulate interstate commerce was given a seemingly limitless reach in the decades after the New Deal. Recent decisions of the Supreme Court have reasserted that obvious definitional premise—that a subject cannot be interstate if it does not relate in some reasonably direct way to things that move across state lines. The same reasoning should apply with still more rigor to international legal commitments: they must have some reasonably close connection to something that actually crosses international borders.

The second rule is that a treaty or international *agreement* must involve genuine *reciprocity* in the obligations it imposes on each side. Like the requirement that treaties be genuinely international, the requirement of reciprocity follows from the nature or purpose of the treaty power. Here, again, is an obvious analogy with recent rulings on interstate commerce. The Supreme Court has insisted that the power to regulate interstate commerce must be limited to matters genuinely related to commerce, since the Constitution grants that regulatory power for the purpose of protecting *commerce*.[11] By like reasoning, one can see that treaties must have some genuine element of reciprocity, since the power to make international commitments was granted in the Constitution to secure concessions or benefits from other countries. As *The Federalist* explained, "[A] treaty is only another name for a bargain." In other words, "treaties . . . are *contracts* with foreign nations which have the force of law."[12]

The commitments on each side need not be parallel or equal. No one supposes that every treaty must, as a matter of constitutional law, amount to a good "bargain" for the United States. But to qualify as a constitutional exercise of the treaty power, a treaty must secure some reasonably specific and enforceable concession or commitment from the other country or countries involved. Otherwise, the treaty becomes simply a vehicle to impose a new policy on the United States, which is plainly an abuse of the power to make treaties.[13]

Many treaties that seem to deal with internal matters will still satisfy those two rules. Some of our earliest treaty commitments, for example, established the right of nationals from particular countries to own or inherit land in American territory. Though the land in question might be entirely within our borders, the foreign owners crossed international borders to take possession (or sent money across international borders to secure ownership rights). And the underlying obligations in those treaties were entirely reciprocal. The United States promised particular countries to protect land claims by their nationals in return for promises by those countries to protect the property claims of American nationals in their territory.[14] In principle, the legal commitment (at least regarding future claimants) might be withdrawn, if France or Mexico reneged on its promise to honor the same policy within its territory.[15]

Yet neither of those criteria for legitimate treaties—that they be truly international and truly reciprocal—is satisfied by contemporary human rights conventions. Those conventions purport to commit the United States to observe certain standards in its treatment of its own citizens within its own territory. In principle, other signatories promise to observe the same standards in their treatment of their citizens. But nothing here is international. The conventions purport to establish standards that each country would apply in its own territory, even if nobody ever moved from one nation to the next. Nothing need cross a border for the conventions to operate.

Nor is there any real reciprocity. Suppose that we ratified the Convention on the Elimination of Discrimination against Women and then enacted an ambitious policy of comparable-worth regulation to implement that obligation within that treaty. Suppose, then, we discover that Angola, Bangladesh, Vietnam, or Iraq—to pick a few states from well over a hundred that have ratified this treaty—are not honoring their commitment to do likewise. Then what? Would we discontinue our own comparable-worth regulation to retaliate on them? There is no way to disentangle the share of that policy that is undertaken in reciprocity for actions by those wretched countries any more than for Australia, Sweden, or Germany—signatories that do have such policies. In fact, nothing we do to implement that treaty can, in any serious way, be regarded as an inducement to others to do the same. It is at best a system of "parallel play," to use the nursery school term.

It is sometimes said that human rights conventions are designed to "legislate" universal standards, so the issue of reciprocity is irrelevant. But that is just the point. The treaty power does not authorize the U.S. government to make international legislation but to make "contracts" or "bargains" on behalf of the United States. The difference is hardly semantic. If one party to a contract defaults on his obligations, the other party is released from his own contractual duties. If one person violates a legislative enactment, that gives no one else the right to break that same law. The honest citizen is not released from his duty to the law by the criminality of others, because the law is there to benefit the whole community and not any particular citizen. Contracts do cease in their obligation when one side defaults because they are precisely about achieving mutual benefit to the parties. And the traditional view was that American treaties were, in that sense, contracts.[16]

That does not mean that the United States cannot participate in multilateral treaties. Even multilateral treaties can often be conceived as bargains or contracts among the parties. One country's default may not impair the obligations that complying nations still have toward each other, though it cancels their obligations (regarding adherence to the common standard) toward the nation that fails to comply. Human rights conventions, however, cannot be conceived as multilateral bargains of that sort: our obligations to Iraq or Bangladesh, under the Women's Rights Convention, are not, in any meaningful sense, affected by those countries' failure to live up to its terms, since the treaty is not in any serious way about *mutual* obligations. There is simply no real connection between what Iraq does to its citizens and what the United States does to its citizens because nothing is exchanged in that convention.

So, if we take the traditional and logical criteria seriously, human rights conventions are not legitimate treaties for the United States. The United States certainly can—as it often has in recent decades—impose various financial sanctions or other penalties on regimes that practice brutal repression. We can even cite the rhetoric of UN human rights conventions, if we cannot find our own words to denounce the practices we most deplore. As a practical matter, our own unilateral actions are likely to have more immediate effect and do more to alleviate human suffering than does any of the rhetoric emanating from the United Nations. Meanwhile, Congress or state legislatures can always adopt as a matter of internal American policy any standards from those conventions that happen to appeal to Americans (and are actually constitutional). But a fair reading of the U.S. Constitution suggests that we cannot bind ourselves to any contemporary human rights convention as a bona fide exercise of the treaty power.

By now, after so many decades of active U.S. participation in the drafting of those conventions, that conclusion may appear somewhat startling, as if it were an unanticipated or inadvertent encumbrance, suddenly rediscovered in a long-forgotten title deed. The truth is that the old restrictions on the treaty power were consciously deprecated or obscured by prominent commentators precisely to make human rights conventions seem to be legitimate. Louis Henkin, the chief reporter for the Third *Restatement* (and a leading proponent of its doctrine that the treaty power has no subject-matter limits), has recently acknowledged that international human rights law is "revolutionary" in its origins, that it has "shaken the sources of international law, reshaped its character, enlarged its domain," and that it is "all new law, at most half a century old." International human rights law is all those things, Henkin affirms, precisely because it reaches into the internal affairs of states with no real international predicate.[17] In fact, the novelty of those conventions required a new understanding of what international law was about or how it would operate.[18] Henkin has thus characterized the emerging international law of human rights as a "constitutional law" for a new era in international affairs.[19] The characterization deserves some respect, not only in view of Henkin's eminence but also because the relevant "law" is otherwise difficult to categorize or explain. But if one accepts the characterization, one cannot evade the question it poses: does the U.S. Constitution really permit the United States to deploy its own lawmaking or treaty-making powers to make "constitutional law" for the world—a law that ultimately must present itself as, in some sense, paramount to our own Constitution?

Revitalizing Constitutional Limits on the Treaty Power

If the better view is that the treaty power does have limits, how would those limitations be enforced? Despite dicta in older cases, courts have been reluctant to become entangled in disputes about foreign policy. No treaty has ever been held void for violating the Constitution. Some cases have interpreted treaties narrowly to avoid constitutional problems.[20] Others have struck down implementing measures as in violation of the Constitution, without actually questioning the underlying international agreement.[21] But as most of the new regulatory treaties do not have direct effect in American law, few have ever been subject to direct constitutional challenge in the courts. Most implementing legislation does not even turn on the validity of a prior treaty:

much of our trade legislation, for example, can stand on its own whether we view it as implementing a binding international commitment or simply as a unilateral American stance.

But it remains true that even when a properly presented case arises, courts are deferential to executive leadership in foreign affairs.[22] That is a long-established pattern and, for many reasons, a quite defensible one. It is not true, however, that the paucity of litigation and the general culture of judicial deference in that area leave constitutional limitations here with no force or no future. Even limitations that courts do not enforce can have a powerful effect. That is the only conclusion to draw from the trajectory of debate over presidential war powers in the course of the twentieth century.

As late as the fall of 1941, while President Roosevelt was striving to give all possible aid to Britain and Russia, he did not dare to deploy American troops or ships into direct offensive operations without a declaration of war. By 1950, with the United Nations regarded as the guarantor of international security, President Truman asserted the power to send a half million troops to Korea on the sole say-so of the UN Security Council. Truman did not seek a declaration of war or any lesser form of direct authorization from Congress, and Congress did not insist on a direct say in the matter. Fifteen years later, President Johnson began a still larger and longer commitment of troops to the war in Vietnam—again with no declaration of war and no serious, direct authorization from Congress. But debate thereafter made a deep impression. By 1990, President Bush, though armed with authorization from the UN Security Council, still insisted on securing formal authorization from Congress before launching offensive operations in the Persian Gulf.[23]

So assumptions about presidential war powers swelled to new heights in the first decade after World War II and then dwindled back to their historic bounds in the decades after Vietnam—and all without a single direct decision by the Supreme Court, without any binding rulings by lower courts, without much judicial precedent even from earlier times.[24]

It is true, of course, that the constitutional debate did not occur in a vacuum. In 1974, amid bitter recriminations at the end of the Vietnam War, Congress enacted the War Powers Resolution, setting strict time limits on the deployment of American forces into war zones without direct congressional approval. Every president since then has denied that this measure is constitutionally binding, and successive presidents have found various ways to evade its apparent restrictions. But the climate of presidential decision-making—and of congressional reactions—has undoubtedly been changed. General arguments have had a general effect on the atmosphere.

The atmosphere was not simply transformed by appeals to constitutional history and logic. Of course, the debacle in Vietnam was much more important in changing opinion. But it made a difference that critics had already begun to develop arguments against presidential overreaching before the change of opinion on the war in Vietnam. And the arguments have had some lasting effect, even as subsequent history has rearranged the political constellations of the Vietnam era debate. Whatever its deficiencies as a comprehensive regulatory scheme, the War Powers Resolution has had lasting impact as a memorable expression of opposition to unlimited presidential war powers.

The Challenge to Congress

From that perspective, Congress might go far in revitalizing constitutional limitations on the treaty power simply by refusing to ratify a major treaty that exceeds those limitations and making such constitutional objections the cornerstone of its opposition. But Congress might usefully go further. The easiest and clearest legislative action would be a measure to forestall abuses of customary international law (of the sort described in chapter 5). All Congress has to do is enact a statute excluding application of customary international law in American courts, at least in cases regarding the conduct of U.S. citizens.

A different statute might curb other abuses by establishing a procedural framework—a sort of international extension to the Administrative Procedure Act—to set limits on when and how the United States can subscribe to international regulatory standards by U.S. executive agreement. Military and security arrangements, if they have no direct effect in U.S. domestic law, might be exempted from such a statute. Congress might still establish that applications or elaborations of treaties in other fields cannot be adopted (for the United States) by unilateral executive action without some procedural safeguards.

Beyond such statutory reforms, it may be equally appropriate for Congress to propose a formal amendment to the Constitution, clarifying limits on the treaty power, so that even future Senates will be warned against ratifying the sort of open-ended or improper international commitment that strains the logic of the Constitution. An amendment might also clarify limits on presidential power to bind the United States by executive agreement (alike in cases where they are authorized by prior legislation or treaty, as in cases where such agreements claim authority from distinct constitutional powers of the executive).

Whether a formal constitutional amendment could be adopted—or fully enforced in the future—is certainly open to question. But it may not be crucial, in any case. Simply in launching a debate on the matter, Congress would greatly alter the atmosphere of international policy. In the early 1950s, a substantial majority of the Senate—though one vote shy of the required two-thirds majority—endorsed a constitutional amendment proposed by Senator John Bricker of Ohio. It would have provided that no treaty or executive agreement could have binding effect without implementing legislation and that no such legislation could be enacted unless it would be constitutional to do so, even in the absence of a treaty. Chief among the targets of the Bricker Amendment, as its sponsors openly acknowledged, were the human rights conventions then being developed by the United Nations. Critics feared that without such an amendment, adoption of those treaties would allow executive officials to impose (or license Congress to enact) domestic policies violating the Bill of Rights and invading the reserved powers of the states.

Whether or not those fears were exaggerated,[25] the point to notice is that the proposed amendment gave tremendous force to such concerns. The Eisenhower administration, while arguing that the Bricker Amendment was too restrictive in other ways, conceded that the critics had a point. Secretary of State Dulles promised not to commit the United States to any UN human rights convention. For a generation thereafter—a period extending through four subsequent administrations—no president did.

Perhaps no simple formula can delineate the limits on permissible international commitments with mechanical precision. But the underlying concerns are not likely to go away. Congress, which bears the ultimate responsibility for lawmaking, is the best place to initiate and direct a debate on how far international commitments can determine American law. Are there no constitutional limits on what the United States can commit itself to do by treaty? If there are limits, do they not constrain the delegation to foreign bodies of lawmaking and law-implementing authority within the United States? Do those limits not also apply, at some point, to the U.S. executive branch, even when it acts as partner or medium for the transmission of international decisions into American law? Do not those limits impose constraints, as well, on the permissible subject matter of international commitments? If not the limits sketched at the outset of this chapter, what limits can be articulated and defended? If the United States will not stand up for its own constitutional system, can we really feel comfortable leaving the Constitution to the vagaries of international negotiation?

If we can focus on the questions, we are not likely to want for reasonably adequate answers. But Congress must be ready to bring the questions into focus. Sooner or later— and hopefully sooner—Congress must launch a serious debate on the constitutional issues.

7

The Standards Applied:
Chasing Global Warming or
Chilling Global Trade?

I f there is to be a debate on the permissible scope of international commitments, the likeliest occasion in the near future will come when the Senate considers the Kyoto Protocol. That agreement was negotiated at the conference of the parties to the Framework Convention on Global Warming, held in Kyoto, Japan, in December 1997. It is, by almost every criterion, a disturbing challenge to constitutional limitations on the treaty power.

The Kyoto Protocol

The heart of the Kyoto Protocol is a series of commitments to cut emission of greenhouse gases over the next fifteen years. Since the principal greenhouse gas is carbon dioxide, which is released by the burning of fossil fuels—coal, oil, and natural gas—the protocol implies substantial cutbacks in energy use. But the details are immensely complicated and again and again are delegated to subsequent meetings or to specialized expert bodies, such as the Intergovernmental Panel on Climate Change, the Subsidiary Body for Scientific and Technological Advice, the "clean development mechanism," and other operational entities. Under the protocol, thirty-nine "developed" countries commit themselves to specified levels of reduction in emissions. Each will make an assessment of its own emissions, then monitor and report to international authorities on its progress toward those targets—as measured and assessed by rules to be clarified in the future.

At the same time, the listed countries commit to "modalities, rules and guidelines" as to how and which additional "human-induced activities related to changes in greenhouse gas emissions and removals in agricultural soil and land use change and forestry categories shall be added to or subtracted from."[1] In plainer English, countries may offset increased emissions by expanding forest "sinks," which draw carbon dioxide from the atmosphere. But reductions in such reabsorption from changed land-use practices may in turn be counted against the offsets when calculating total progress toward the reduction targets. How all of that will be measured and credited is deferred to future meetings and expert rulings. So, too, the protocol allows countries to offset some of their own reduction obligations by sponsoring emission-reduction efforts in less-developed countries—but only when the reduction would not otherwise be made and only when the venture meets with the approval of the "clean development mechanism," a standing bureaucratic appendage to the conference of the parties.[2]

Without belaboring the details, we can see that a great many policy issues have been left open for future determination. The Kyoto Protocol does not specify how many of those issues will be clarified in additional protocols, subject to separate ratification by the participating states. The U.S. Senate ought to consider that question, however. It might make a large difference, after all, how various "technical" questions are decided. Whether the value of new forest sinks, for example—or the trade-off value of sponsored reductions in other countries—is calculated by one rule or a competing rule may literally spell hundreds of billions of dollars difference in added savings or added burdens to the U.S. economy. How much of that can we sensibly leave to determination by foreign representatives or established international experts? It will not be feasible to package all the emerging "technical" rules into a subsequent protocol, but it remains unclear whether any of them will be. If not, a single act of ratification would seem to be committing the United States to a vast amount of subsequent policy decision by foreigners.

Apart from its implementing mechanisms, the substance of the Kyoto Protocol also raises serious questions. Essentially, the protocol commits the United States to reduce its own energy consumption within its own borders. How does fuel consumption by motorists in Kansas or homeowners in Minnesota affect other countries? We are not talking about effects as direct as water pollution flowing between the United States and Mexico or air pollution drifting between the United States and Canada. The connection between the subjects of the treaty and actual international exchange—border crossing—is not even so direct as in the Montreal Protocol on chlorofluorocarbon use, where chemical compounds released into the atmosphere in other countries were thought to have a relatively immediate effect on ozone concentrations over northern parts of the United States. The cause-and-effect claims here are far more remote and tenuous: more carbon dioxide emissions may contribute to atmospheric buildups that may contribute to a warming trend, which may have disturbing effects on weather patterns fifty or a hundred years hence.[3]

Even if the cause and effect are thought to be close enough to establish a properly international pattern, the greatest weakness remains. The agreement has no serious reciprocity. In fact, the protocol offers no specific enforcement mechanism at all. There is no way to determine what harm is done when any particular signatory fails to reach its emission-reduction targets in the appointed period—or fails to accept the determination of international inspectors or international authorities that it has so failed. We cannot renege on our commitment to any particular country that fails in its commitment. Are we released from our overall obligations if a sizable number of other signatories (but less than a majority, perhaps) fail in theirs?

The underlying problem, however, is even more serious than the problem of individual delinquents: the majority of countries have not committed to any emission reductions, and that majority—which includes such developing giants as China, India, and Brazil—will soon account for the greater part of the world's greenhouse gas emissions.[4] So we have good reason to fear that the entire effort will prove futile, even in its own terms, as emission reductions made by the United States and other developed nations are offset by still larger emission increases by newly industrializing nations. Such countries actually have strong incentives both to demand continuing effort from the developing world and to shirk any controls on their own development, since such asymmetrical obligations will spur relocation of industry from developed countries to those without controls. Developing countries may well think that, given the desperate poverty with which they now contend, the risks from some degree of global warming in future decades are more than compensated for by gains from more rapid growth today.[5] If global warming does prove a problem, after all, richer countries will be better able to cope with whatever environmental stresses it may bring.

In such circumstances, it is fair to wonder whether we can consider the Kyoto Protocol a genuine treaty—a meaningful contract between the United States and other nations—or simply a grandiose display of concern about "the environment."[6] Diplomats have promised more clarification of details, including the future obligations of less developed countries, when the parties to the Framework Convention on Climate Change meet again in Buenos Aires at the end of 1998. In the meantime, policies to induce more efficient fuel use within the United States may well have other justifications, apart from the particular program contemplated by the Kyoto Protocol. But if our policies are to be premised on an international "obligation," it is not too early to ask how and to what extent that obligation is really obligatory—and whether the obligation is consistent with the Constitution. If commitments become more painful in the future, it will be well to clarify in advance how far we understand ourselves to be bound and truly committed. One need not, at any rate, deny the possibility of long-term danger in global warming to conclude that the United States cannot now—given the limits imposed by the Constitution—commit itself to the Kyoto Protocol.

We might do quite a few things in the meanwhile. The United States can certainly cooperate in international research to clarify the true scale of the danger. There is certainly no constitutional problem in imposing emission limitations within the United States, in hopes that other countries will follow our example. There is no inherent constitutional problem in making unilateral American offers of financial and technical assistance to other countries to reduce their emissions. We might even negotiate acceptable treaties with individual countries, by which the American government would provide tax credits or other incentives to American business to undertake emission-limiting investments in the affected countries, so long as those countries undertake to ensure that U.S. investments are not offset by emission increases by other industries within their borders (on pain of losing the assist to U.S. investments, if they do not). If we find ways of reducing concentrations of greenhouse gases by releasing offsetting chemical agents into the atmosphere, the United States could certainly provide technological and material assistance to such a venture. All such measures are quite different, in constitutional terms, from subscribing to a continuing international regulatory venture, involving delegations of standard-setting and supervisory powers to international agencies, long-term commitments on a range of basic domestic policies, and little assurance that other countries will abide by the terms of the agreement, even if we do.

Those who doubt the adequacy of such approaches may finally have to reckon with the truth that not all problems have adequate responses—given limitations on what we are actually able or prepared to do. Many people, after all, think that population growth will pose great strains on the earth's "carrying capacity" in fifty or a hundred years, quite apart from the effect on greenhouse gas emissions. Numerous UN conferences and research undertakings have called attention to the problem. But no one has seriously advocated an international treaty system by which countries commit themselves to limit their population growth to specific, targeted limits. Certainly, it is hard to conceive that the United States could constitutionally commit itself to such an international control system—among other reasons, because the U.S. Constitution is understood to set real limits on what the American government can do, even on its own initiative, to control the choices that Americans make about childbearing. We cannot always do what some forecasters see as "necessary." Not the least function of the Constitution, after all, is to set limits on the extent to which basic governing principles can be hostage to the demands of policy experts wielding alarms about distant perils.

If we do acknowledge constitutional limitations on the permissible scope of U.S. treaty commitments, does that mean that the United States can never really commit itself to international projects of major importance? In many areas, in fact, the limitations and concerns sketched in the preceding chapters need not be a barrier to effective international cooperation.

GATT, WTO, and NAFTA

Probably the single most effective and consequential international program of the postwar era has been the mutual reduction of trade barriers under the General Agreement on Tariffs and Trade, initiated in 1947. Reasonable questions may be raised about certain aspects of the World Trade Organization, established in 1995 to help administer GATT norms. But, fundamentally, the trading system is quite compatible with traditional notions of sovereignty. It was developed on the foundations of much older sorts of international agreement, which would have been quite recognizable to the Framers of the Constitution.

To start with, trading rules formalized in successive GATT rounds focus precisely on those goods (and now services) that cross international boundaries. Under current GATT rules, the way goods are produced inside the exporting country cannot be a concern of the importing country. Each country agrees to lower barriers on goods entering its own borders and to ignore what other countries do within their own borders in making those goods.

Second, the fundamental ground of the system is reciprocity. In other words, the underlying structure of trade agreements is genuinely contractual. The fact that GATT rounds are multilateral agreements is not essential to their character. In essence, GATT rounds are a series of bargains: we reduce trade barriers on our side in return for parallel reductions by other countries. The bargain can be enforced one-on-one. We can retaliate against any country that has, in our view, failed to honor its trade policy commitment to the United States. The main purpose of the new dispute-settling machinery under the WTO is to focus and limit disputes to ensure that retaliation does not escalate into a generalized trade war.

As the GATT has proceeded from agreements to lower import duties to agreements to reduce nontariff barriers, it has allowed questions to be raised about various kinds of import restrictions. In general, the rules require that countries apply the same health and safety standards to imports as to domestic products. Although there is no requirement that all WTO members adhere to the same regulatory standards, efforts have been made to ensure that countries do not contrive safety or health concerns as a mere pretext for excluding imports. In one trade dispute, Japan claimed that American-made snow skis had to be excluded for safety reasons, because snow in Japan was different from the snow in North America. A GATT panel found that the asserted safety claim was an improper trade barrier. While consumer advocates have objected to that feature of the GATT system—from fear that it exposes American safety standards to challenge by other countries—it is hard to see that any serious constitutional problem exists with that aspect of the trade system. We submit to restrictions in return for similar restrictions on other countries, with all of that hinging on products that cross our borders.

The WTO may raise some constitutional questions about delegation in two ways. The first is that by submitting disputes to arbitration panels, we are implicitly allowing the terms of our obligation—as applied to the details of a specific policy—to be determined by international authority, rather than by American ratification. But not every submission to international arbitration is inherently unconstitutional: such submissions have been an element of American statecraft since the 1790s, when the Jay Treaty with Britain arranged for an international panel to arbitrate property disputes arising from the American Revolution. In fact, the United States was one of the most insistent champions of formal arbitration in the negotiations to establish the WTO. The United States has been eager to secure authoritative judgments in challenges to the protectionist policies of other countries.

One might argue that the acceptability of such dispute-settling mechanisms turns on their sticking closely to the logic of existing agreements. If the panels end up building an ambitious "case law" that elaborates a whole new set of obligations with questionable support in the existing agreement, we might come to think of the WTO as establishing a new authority that in practice has changed the meaning of that to which we actually agreed. Because the WTO operates with ad hoc panels and with shifting personnel, there is less likelihood that the panels will try to build up an ambitious law of precedents in the manner of life-tenured judges on a permanent court. At any rate, having more settled rules is a central object of our trade policy, so the panels ought to be given at least some deference in hopes that other countries will also accept panel rulings.

A potentially more serious question exists regarding the new amending procedure for trade rules. Before the inauguration of the WTO in 1995, participating countries committed themselves to a package of new rules—all at once. In effect, the GATT established a trading club, with successive rounds of agreement, all of them duly ratified by all the member states, adding new rules for the club. Individual members could then accept the whole new package to stay within the club or walk away. The agreement establishing the WTO provides that an amendment or a separate new rule can be added by a two-thirds vote of the members but will only bind those member states that do agree to the new rule. In special cases, a new rule can be imposed even on members that object to it, leaving them the choice of submitting to the new rule or exiting the club altogether. Such impositions can only be imposed, however, by a three-quarters majority of existing members.

As a practical matter, the United States is most unlikely to be on the losing side of a three-quarters vote. Among other things, a three-quarters majority is hard to obtain in international negotiations (as it is in congressional votes) when the subject is actually contentious. As the world's largest trading nation, moreover, the United States is unlikely to be expelled from a club that would lose half its value to the other members if the United States were not a member.

Meanwhile, the WTO remains international in the true and traditional sense: it is an arrangement for coordinating policies between governments about goods and services that cross national borders. The commitments made in GATT rounds are implemented by domestic legislation. Domestic courts enforce only such domestic implementing legislation. The international dispute-settling machinery is available only for government-to-government disputes. If American firms are dissatisfied with American trade policy, they must take their complaints to the American government. They have no direct recourse to the WTO, nor do foreign firms, which can reach the WTO only by persuading their own governments to raise objections against an American policy. In no case can the WTO reach directly into U.S. domestic law or impose a change in American law that American political authorities do not approve.

In that respect, the WTO presents fewer constitutional problems than NAFTA. In the NAFTA scheme, the fundamental terms of the agreement do rest on congressional legislation: there is no question of a NAFTA panel's directly imposing a new regulatory requirement on American firms. But at least with respect to countervailing duties (to punish dumping of foreign goods, below their true cost), private firms have direct access to arbitration panels, and American courts must enforce the panel decisions without any independent review. In that small respect, NAFTA has a self-executing quality that allows policy actions by American officials (in imposing specific duties) to be directly overturned, without any subsequent policy review by American officials. It is, perhaps, a small deviation from the proper constitutional scheme that American courts may yet correct—or hold unconstitutional. But that aspect of NAFTA is not at any rate a precedent we should be willing to extend.

Proposed Linkage Policies

NAFTA also presents a different problem not present in WTO norms. In special side accords, each country in NAFTA has promised not to cut back on enforcing its existing environmental protections or on certain specified protections for labor.[7] The obligation covers only those national standards that each member state has already adopted for its own purposes. Even then, lack of enforcement can only be challenged when it is alleged to affect the competitive position of products in cross-border trade. And the challenge must be routed to a special commission that has cumbersome procedures designed to encourage compromise before a final decision is reached. The ultimate penalty for infraction of the side accords is an imposition of special tariffs, with the proceeds designated for a fund to enhance regulatory enforcement in the country complained against.

None of that is likely to make a major difference in itself. It has nonetheless established a precedent that remains disturbing—especially if it is extended into the WTO, as some advocates have urged.[8] The problem is that the rationale for the NAFTA side accords can be expanded without limit. The argument for the side accords was that if one country failed to enforce environmental or labor regulations on its own business firms, it might give those firms a competitive advantage in dealing with firms of the other countries, which would still have to comply with costly regulatory requirements. By the same logic, however, one can argue that firms receive an improper advantage when national standards in their own country, even if fully enforced, are less demanding in their substantive requirements than the standards in place in the neighboring countries. So, by that argument, there ought to be common standards (and not just commitments from each country to enforce its own separate national standards, such as they may be). Similarly, NAFTA links the enforcement of environmental and labor standards to export industries. The same logic might suggest that standards should be harmonized and fully enforced across the entire national economy. Otherwise, it may be argued, cost reductions for suppliers of components and providers of services to exporting firms will lower total costs for the latter, even if the exporting firms themselves must adhere to international standards.

Extending the logic of the NAFTA side accords is exactly what the Clinton administration—and many environmental and labor advocates—have urged. They have insisted that NAFTA expansion must be accompanied by expansion of the side accords.[9] And they have pushed to have such policies extended to the WTO.[10] Such linkage policies are already central to the workings of the European Union. Germany, as the most affluent and the most "green" of the member states, has insisted that its own ambitious environmental policies (as well as some of its labor protection policies) be extended to all members of the European trade system. In effect, Germany has told Portugal, Greece, and other less affluent countries that they can only achieve privileged access to German markets if they accept German-sponsored standards in their own environmental and labor programs.

At present, WTO rules prohibit members from restricting imports simply out of objections to the way the imported products were made in their home country. Less-developed countries have been adamant in their opposition to any modifications of that rule. It may be that, even if the WTO embraces internal production standards, they will have to be so minimal (to win acceptance from less-developed countries) that they will have no effect on the United States.[11] But such standards might be developed by making a distinction between developed and less-developed countries (as was done in the Kyoto Protocol). In that case, advocates of more ambitious regulatory practices in the United States may find allies in Europe, eager to encourage international standards that place burdens on American firms comparable to those on their European counterparts.

Even to enter negotiations on such matters, the United States would have to concede that, to gain trade advantages, it stands ready to revise a wide range of domestic policies to suit the demands of trading partners. Whether a particular practice could be described as a proper subject of international concern would turn on the ambitions of trade partners. Their ambitions may be encouraged, in turn, by the clamors of U.S. political constituencies that are eager to impose such conditions on U.S. firms but lack the strength to do so except through the leverage provided by trade negotiations with foreign governments.

That Greece and Portugal have found it advantageous to make such bargains, however, does not mean that the United States would be well advised to do so or that the U.S. Constitution leaves the United States equally free to do so. U.S. decisions about essentially domestic matters—essentially domestic in that they have only a remote, indirect connection with anything that crosses a border—cannot properly be open to international negotiation. There are limits to what the United States can submit to international bargaining. The Constitution does not allow any and all domestic policies to be bartered for trade advantages. U.S. sovereignty cannot be for sale.

8

American Ideals in a Nonideal World

Everyone remembers the affirmation of "self-evident truths" in the Declaration of Independence—"that all men are created equal, . . . endowed by their Creator with certain unalienable Rights. . . . That to secure these rights, Governments are instituted among Men, deriving their just powers from the consent of the governed." We tend to forget that those famous words appear only in the second paragraph of the Declaration, in explication of the less-remembered assertions of the opening sentence:

> When in the Course of human events, it becomes necessary for one people to dissolve the political bands which have connected them to another, and to assume among the powers of the earth, the separate and equal station to which the Laws of Nature and of Nature's God entitle them, a decent respect to the opinions of mankind requires that they should declare the causes which impel them to the separation.

The opening lines of the Declaration invoke natural law and divine sanction for the principle of national sovereignty. Why are independent nations "entitled" to a "separate and equal station"? First, because—like individuals in a natural state—they have no superior on earth: they are equal in the sense that they are equally free. Any human power claiming an authority above all nations would be putting itself in the place of God. And that is so, in the second place, because governments "draw their just powers from the consent of the governed." Government must therefore be accountable to the governed, not to some higher authority outside.

The wording of the opening paragraph—and much else—implies that the "one people" (later described as "the people") have a bond of connection that precedes government. This formulation is not a mere figure of speech. If one looks to the principal philosophic source for the Declaration of Independence, John Locke's *Treatise of Government*, one finds that the original "social contract" is an agreement to be governed in common—that is, in effect, an agreement to be "one people" for political purposes. Only after that agreement is reached can "the people" determine what form of government they will have.[1] The prior agreement to act as one people makes it possible to posit that "the people," as a more or less united force, can then defend themselves against an abusive government. The theory may not fit neatly with the circumstances of the American colonial revolt, but the final text of the Declaration deliberately glossed over the complications.[2] Without some notion of a preexisting "people," revolution would be either a practical impossibility or a conspiracy of the few against the rest.

One can see the point from a different angle by thinking through the Declaration's assertion that the "just powers" of government derive from "the consent of the governed." No one ever supposed that government by consent would require every government action to receive unanimous public approval. At best, one cannot expect more than majority support. It is not even reasonable to expect unanimous agreement on the constitutionally prescribed procedure for making policy. But to feel obligated by the decision of the requisite majority in the framing of a constitution, one must already accept the necessity or appropriateness of living under the same system with those others who make that majority. When we speak of America as a democracy, we imply that government is accountable to the majority—but the majority of our own people. For there to be a democracy, there must first be a demos—a distinct people.[3]

Many writers now insist that such views are outdated in a world that is so much more "interdependent." But the same arguments were once supposed to be powerful objections to private property and individual liberty in a modern economy. The truth, now acknowledged by virtually all reputable economists, is quite the reverse: the complexity of the modern world makes it all the more necessary to leave owners to determine how their resources and efforts can best be deployed. Historically, the argument for national sovereignty was closely connected with parallel arguments for private property.[4]

Certainly, we need collective authority to punish and deter aggression. It would be a strong argument for international authority, if it could actually punish and deter aggression among nations, as government police forces do among individuals in domestic settings. But sovereign states are not willing to entrust such supreme authority to the United Nations, so we find that international organization does little to punish or deter aggression—whether in the mangled streets of Sarajevo or in the fiendish weapons laboratories of Iraq. Instead of facing those most urgent challenges, we gratify the collectivist impulse with international agreements on other subjects. Some contemporary agreements are, in fact, nothing else but sheer monuments to collectivist ideology. Is it plausible that the world at large cares more about the wildlife treasures of Africa or the art treasures of Europe—or, indeed, the national parks of America—than do the sovereign states that derive tourist dollars and many other benefits from protecting those national resources within their own borders? Plausible or not, that is the necessary premise of such ventures as the UN's World Heritage Convention.

Many people will agree that sovereignty must remain an important principle in the modern world, but then go on to argue that it must be given new definitions and should not, in any case, be defined in dogmatic or legalistic terms.[5] In the contemporary world, we are told, the artificial interests of states must give way to the common yearnings of mankind. And almost everyone with a modicum of decency does find something affecting in calls to recover our common humanity. But such affecting sentiments do not provide a workable plan of government.

Higher Powers

The truth is that calls to a higher human duty, transcending the interest of particular nations, are not a novelty of the twentieth century. Something like that vision is quite old. In fact, it is medieval. The most hopeful thinkers of medieval Europe emphasized that, beyond the quarrels and ambitions of rival kings and princes, there remained an underlying unity of Christendom, which should in time embrace all the world. The trouble with this vision was that such transcending unity, even on the spiritual plane, was impossible to maintain without a common authority. The effort to maintain the spiritual supremacy of the church turned out to add simply one more occasion for bloodshed and division. The doctrine of sovereignty was invented in the sixteenth and seventeenth centuries with the precise purpose of denying that human authorities, enforcing a higher law on the supreme authority within each state, could maintain the unity of Christendom. The exponents of sovereignty did not deny the truths of religion or of transcendent doctrines. They simply insisted that no human power could enforce those claims on independent states. Our own Declaration of Independence picks up the theme: independent nations are equal before God, but not subordinate to any human authority.

That is not the stuff of remote history but of contemporary American politics. Almost all public figures acknowledge that our government has moral duties, apart from what voters might prefer at any moment. But let someone assert that American government should be subject to some particular religious authority and cries of protest will be furious and unrelenting. Suppose, for example, that an earnest congressman sought to "protect our moral values" by requiring that all new federal regulations touching on sensitive "moral issues" be submitted for advance comment to the Vatican. He could offer to make his bill more palatable by stipulating that the pope's comments would only be "advisory" and then stipulate that the archbishop of Canterbury, the chief rabbi of Jerusalem, and the Dalai Lama of Tibet be included in the consultation. If it is possible to conceive such a law's being enacted, it remains impossible to imagine that the law would escape a prompt constitutional challenge from advocates of "separation of church and state."[6] The challenge would turn on a question that most commentators would acknowledge as a true question of *principle.*[7]

What we refuse to consider for religious authority, however, we have started to do quite routinely with foreign governments. We share some of our governing authority with them, by making them partners in our domestic concerns. We see the necessity to guard and clarify the proper boundaries between government and religion, but we have come to think it is not important to guard or clarify the proper boundaries between our government and other governments, or between our own government and international organizations in which it participates.

With regard to religion, no one denies that legitimate issues of principle about church and state can exist—even though the United States does not face the danger of sliding down a slippery slope to a national theocracy. Surely, a big part of the reason is that we are concerned as much about what happens at the top of the slope as at some speculative precipice further down the slide. We do not want religious disputes to poison our politics. So we try to exclude potentially divisive issues turning directly on religion. Yet we have experienced, throughout the twentieth century, an undercurrent of suspicion and resentment toward the United Nations (and before that, the League of Nations) as a potential world government, threatening to American sovereignty. That is in many ways the contemporary counterpart of antipopery crusades in the nineteenth century. Our way of dealing with the latter was to insist that the Catholic faith could not pose any danger of dual loyalties in a republic based on separation of church and state. Our way of dealing with fear of international organization, through much of the twentieth century, was to insist that we would tolerate no threat to American sovereignty. That was said with much emphasis in the 1950s but is not so clearly or fully affirmed today.[8]

Separation of church and state is not simply a principle we embrace to ward off theocracy or even to ward off nasty political conflicts. One of America's finest achievements has been to create a space for stable, democratic politics. Constitutional limitations, by removing some issues from political debate, have helped to safeguard the underlying consensus on which a vigorous but stable democracy depends. Removing sectarian authority from politics has strengthened democracy, but so also has a prior insistence on defending national sovereignty.

The Supreme Court has, of course, been quite active in recent decades in interpreting and enforcing the constitutional doctrine prohibiting "establishment of religion." By contrast, the Court has tended to shy away from constitutional disputes touching on foreign policy. Yet, as noted in chapter 6, we have had an extended debate about presidential war powers in recent decades that seems to have established renewed respect for congressional prerogatives in committing the country to war. The war powers debate proceeded with almost no assistance from the courts. In fact, the country had extended debates over church-state issues in the nineteenth century—so that, for example, Congress for some years insisted on Sunday mail delivery to avoid any hint of endorsement for the Christian sabbath—and pursued such debates with no guidance from the Supreme Court.

Defending the American View

It is true that other countries do not always display great devotion to American notions about sovereignty. It is also true that in 1776 few countries accepted the doctrines of self-government and human equality proclaimed in the Declaration of Independence. To claim that a particular doctrine is "universal" in its validity does not require proof that it is universally accepted. The United States must decide for itself how it will interpret and safeguard its own sovereignty.

The United States has always taken a somewhat equivocal view of international commitments. Today, the United States takes an unusual position on many issues of international law and international cooperation. We are one of the only countries—certainly one of the only Western countries—to refuse to subscribe to major UN human rights conventions or to almost any labor standards established by the ILO. We are also one of the few countries that has refused to endorse the UN's Convention on the Law of the Sea and that has opposed the new proposal for an international criminal court.

We should consider two further points before we let the practices of other countries raise doubts about the proper view of sovereignty for the United States. First, different countries often define general principles somewhat differently, and we rarely take the different approaches as a signal to change our own ways. For example, although most of the world now gives at least some rhetorical support to democracy, most genuine democracies have adopted a parliamentary system rather than the American presidential system, with its sharper separation of powers. No one seriously argues that the United States must adapt to the world trend, simply because the scheme of the Framers has not been widely copied. No one thinks that the United States must rethink its own version of separation of church and state because Britain and other countries have managed to combine religious freedom with an established church. So, again, the fact that many other countries are willing to compromise their own sovereignty is not, in itself, a particularly good argument for following their example.

The more important point is that the United States is not a typical country. As the strongest and richest country in the world, the United States can afford to safeguard its sovereignty even if other countries think they cannot do so. An America that stands aloof from various international undertakings will not find that it is thereby shut out from the wider world. On the contrary, we have every reason to expect that other nations, eager for access to American markets and eager for other cooperative arrangements with the United States, will often adapt themselves to American preferences. The United Nations and the World Trade Organization probably would not exist at all if the United States had refused to join them. So, too, most of the major international environmental agreements of recent decades would not be in place if the United States had not supported them.

The United States cannot expect to remake the world in its own image, but it does have great influence in the world. If the United States renews its commitment to safeguarding its own sovereignty, it will not be repudiating or turning its back on the world but rather encouraging other countries to return to their own earlier patterns. Until quite recent decades, international law—and not merely American constitutional law—was premised on an underlying respect for national sovereignty.

In the long run, international law will be stronger if it abandons its most fanciful current pretensions and reverts to the sturdier premises of earlier times. Where international law rests on well-defined, reciprocal commitments about genuinely international matters, international commitments are far more likely to be honored. A world where international obligations are kept within proper bounds may also be a world that offers more encouragement for accountable government and individual rights. At the least, a world where international obligations are kept within proper limits is a world where governments cannot hide behind foreign commitments—or expect international controls or international largesse to rescue their peoples from their own governing failures.

A world with reduced pretensions for international law should also be a world that makes it easier and more likely for people in each country to achieve the level of environmental protection they desire and can afford. Without international controls, less-developed countries will be less likely to adopt the priorities of Western environmentalists, who have been known to display more concern for wildlife than for human welfare and who have enticed poor countries to give more attention to remote atmospheric hazards than to immediately pressing public health problems.

At any rate, America's first duty must be to protect its own democracy and the rights and resources of its own people—by safeguarding its own sovereignty. One need not view that priority as selfish. It is hardly selfish of parents to give first priority to their obligations toward their own children. It is hardly selfish of managers to give first priority to their obligations toward their own firms. It is hardly selfish in those settings to resist outside interference. Asserting a special duty to one's own is not a moral failing. Limiting one's responsibility to what one can reasonably control is not a moral defect. We might describe those responses, in the language of the American Founders, as dictates of the law of nature.

A world in which the United States could safely commit its own domestic policy to international determination would be, in many senses, a different world. The argument for respecting constitutional limits on the scope of such commitments can thus be simply put: the Constitution was made for this world.

Notes

Chapter 1: Getting beyond Slogans

1. For a very careful version of the argument, see John C. Yoo, "The New Sovereignty and the Old Constitution: Chemical Weapons and the Appointments Clause," *Constitutional Commentaries,* vol. 15 (Winter 1997).

2. Opportunistic uses of the term are long-standing and by no means limited to partisans in this country: "Sovereignty is a catch-word which can be used by all and with very different tactical meanings." Stanley Hoffmann, "In Search of a Thread: The UN in the Congo Labyrinth," in David Kay, *United Nations Political Systems* (John Wiley, 1967), p. 257.

3. *Head Money Cases,* 112 U.S. 580 (1884); *Whitney v. Robertson,* 124 U.S. 190 (1888); *Chinese Exclusion Cases,* 130 U.S. 581 (1889).

4. Strange as it may seem, Nazi authorities, too, worried about breaking international law in their treatment of British and American prisoners, because Germany was still a signatory of the relevant Geneva Conventions along with Britain and the United States. During his trial at Nuremberg, General Jodl insisted that regard for that element of international law had led top officials to resist or evade orders from Hitler to execute Allied prisoners, though some executions did still take place. Robert E. Conot, *Justice at Nuremberg* (Carroll & Graf, 1983), pp. 307–18. That was, of course, a special case, with the Western Allies' holding German prisoners as hostage, in effect, to German compliance with the established norms. But it undoubtedly helped to have pre-established norms. As the Soviet Union was not a signatory of the relevant Geneva Conventions, the Germans and the Russians assumed the worst of each other and treated each other's prisoners with horrifying cruelty. Yet even in that most terrible theater

of the war, both Stalin and Hitler did honor the long-established rule against interfering with ambassadors: after the German attack on the Soviet Union, the German Embassy staff in Moscow was allowed to return home without incident, as was the Soviet Embassy staff in Berlin. The wartime achievements of international law may not be much to boast about. Still, its few achievements are worth trying to preserve.

5. So, for example, the ruling of the European Court of Justice in *Regina v. Secretary of State for Transport ex parte Factortame Ltd.* [1990] ECR I-433 held that British courts must invalidate an act of Parliament that conflicts with European Community law—overruling centuries of parliamentary supremacy in one stroke. (See D. Lasok and K. P. E. Lasok, *Law and Institutions of the European Union,* 6th ed. (Butterworths, 1994), pp. 362–64). The authority claimed by European institutions is even more far-reaching, in fact. When Germany's Federal Constitutional Court (FCC) ruled that a particular directive of the European Commission was contrary to Germany's constitution, the European Court of Justice overruled that decision and insisted that the commission be obeyed. *Internationale Handelsgesellschaft MBH v. Einfuhr und Vorratesstelle fur Getreide und Futtermittel,* [1970] E.C.R. 1125. Germany's FCC, itself, eventually acknowledged that it must accept subordinate status to the ECJ, so long as the ECJ incorporated fundamental rights protection into its own jurisprudence (something it had indeed claimed to do, without any clear treaty basis for doing so). For the FCC's opinion, see Judgment of Oct. 22, 1986, 73 BVerfGE 339, translated in [1987] 3 C.M.L.R. 225 (*In Re the Application of Wunsche Handelsgesellschaft.*)

6. North American Free Trade Agreement, reprinted in 32 I.L.M. 289 (1993) Art. 1904. A recent study found that three-quarters of the decided cases under Chapter 19 had been decided unanimously by the panels (so that arbitrators from different countries did not divide on national lines) and most cases were decided within the 315-day time limit. Guillermo Aguilar Alvarez et al., "NAFTA Chapter 19: Binational Panel Review of Antidumping and Countervailing Duty Determinations," in *Trading Punches: Trade Remedy Law and Disputes under NAFTA* (Beatriz Leycegui et al., eds., 1995). The generally satisfactory experience with binational panels under the U.S.-Canada Free Trade Agreement (between 1989 and 1993) may account for the lack of specific controversy about extending the procedure in NAFTA.

Since then, however, there have been three quite acrimonious and protracted disputes on high-value products in U.S.-Canada trade in which panels did divide on national lines (with the United States on the losing side). Mexican officials have complained that antidumping decisions of panels have exceeded their proper authority, while Americans have complained about the slowness of panels in disputes with Mexico. Gustavo Vega-Canovas, "Disciplining Anti-Dumping in North America: Is NAFTA Chapter Nineteen Serving Its Purpose?" *Arizona Journal of International and Comparative Law*, vol. 14 (1997), p. 479.

7. Steven Rhoads, *Incomparable Worth: Pay Equity Meets the Market* (Cambridge University Press, 1993), describes the "legislative history" of the policy within the European Community, where it was strongly championed by France and strongly opposed by the United Kingdom at a meeting of the EC Council of Ministers in the mid-1970s and developed into a major policy commitment only in the early 1980s, when career officials at the European Commission and judges on the European Court of Justice gave a very aggressive interpretation to compromise language adopted by the Council of Ministers—representing the national governments—in the mid-1970s (pp. 130–47). Rhoads presents considerable evidence that major governments would never have agreed to the initial policy if they had known how ambitiously it would later be applied.

8. David Vogel, *Trading Up: Consumer and Environmental Regulation in a Global Economy* (Harvard University Press, 1996) concludes:

> the European Union has been the single most important factor in strengthening national environmental regulations for a number of member states. The European Union has become a vehicle for exporting the environmental standards of Europe's greener nations to the rest of the continent (pp. 96–97).

9. See Martin Rhodes, "A Regulatory Conundrum, Industrial Relations, and the Social Dimension," in Stephen Leibfried and Paul Pierson, eds., *European Social Policy: Between Fragmentation and Integration* (Brookings, 1995): "An impressive corpus of minimum rights has been put in place, not just in the area of health and safety . . . but also in more controversial areas of workers' rights and entitlements" (p. 120). Rhodes notes that disputes on the expansion of such policies have typically developed be-

tween more developed economies in northern Europe and the less-developed nations in southern Europe, with the former inducing the latter to accept higher European standards by promising EU fiscal aid to those countries as an offset to the burdens of compliance with northern regulatory standards. The editors of the volume note that the single-market initiative, negotiated in the mid-1980s to boost European integration, was inspired by "a deregulatory agenda . . . insulated from social policy issues, which would continue to be the bailiwick of the member states." But as things turned out, "the tidy separation between market issues and social issues" has proved "unsustainable" and national governments "have become more and more enmeshed in a complex multitiered web of [Europeanwide] social policy" (pp. 44–45).

10. Alec Stone Sweet and Thomas L. Brunell, "Constructing a Supranational Constitution: Dispute Resolution and Governance in the European Community," *American Political Science Review*, vol. 92 (March 1998), p. 63. Thus, the ECJ has heard 265 cases protesting German policies interfering with the free movement of goods and in the same period has heard 116 such cases against France, 84 against Italy, 86 against the Netherlands, and only 34 against Britain. But in the same period it heard 40 cases about British failure to comply with EU social provisions—four times more than what would have been expected if the cases had been proportionately divided among EU member states on the basis of overall litigation rates (p. 75).

11. Steve Charnowitz, "Governing the Global Economy: Promoting Higher Labor Standards," *Washington Quarterly*, vol. 18 (Summer 1995), p. 167, documents that American support for connecting trade agreements with international labor standards goes back at least to the Eisenhower administration, though the seriousness of such support from successive administrations is open to question.

12. 42 U.S.C. 6295 (k): "(A) Except as provided in subparagraph (B), the maximum water use allowed in gallons per flush for any of the following water closets manufactured after January 1, 1994, is the following: Gravity tank-type toilets 1.6 gpf; Flushometer tank toilets 1.6 gpf; Electromechanical hydraulic toilets 1.6 gpf.; Blowout toilets 3.5 gpf." The specifications on toilets are added to a section of the code headed "Energy Con-

servation Program for Consumer Products Other than Automobiles." They contribute nothing to energy conservation, but probably do not contribute to any other legitimate federal concern, either. Even if they do help to conserve water, it is not likely that saving water in soggier regions will do anything to help irrigate arid regions elsewhere in the country. Someone just seems to have thought national standards for toilets would be a good idea. And manufacturers of plumbing supplies, no doubt, agreed, since they now need not compete on the most basic element of product effectiveness.

Chapter 2: Constitutional Integrity

1. The Constitution, itself, in its final sentence, proclaims that it was "Done in Convention" in the twelfth "Year of . . . the Independence of the United States"—dating American independence to 1776, the year the Declaration of Independence was issued, rather than to 1783, when American independence received formal, international recognition in the Treaty of Paris.

2. *Bowsher v. Synar*, 478 U.S. 714 (1986); *Buckley v. Valeo*, 424 U.S. 1 (1976).

3. "Camillus," in *Works of Alexander Hamilton* (Henry Cabot Lodge, ed., G.P. Putnam's Sons, 1885), vol. 5, p. 30.

4. Among the leading cases are *U.S. v. Curtiss-Wright Export Corp.*, 299 U.S. 304 (1936); *United States v. Belmont*, 301 U.S. 324 (1937); and *Dames & Moore v. Regan*, 453 U.S. 654 (1981).

5. *Missouri v. Holland*, 252 U.S. 416 (1920); *United States v. Belmont*, 301 U.S. 324 (1937).

6. *Geofroy v. Riggs*, 133 U.S. 258, 267 (1890). The Constitution expressly forbids Congress from subdividing the territory of the states without their consent (Art. IV, Sec. 3) but links such action to the erection of new states. To view this restriction as a continuing constraint on the treaty power is a striking tribute to constitutional orthodoxy: surrender of territory was a routine element of peace treaties in the nineteenth century. See, to the same effect, Joseph Story, *Commentaries on the Constitution*, vol. 3, § 1502: (Hilliard, Gray, 1833, reprinted by DaCapo Press, 1970), p. 356: "A treaty to change the organization of the Government, to annihilate its sovereignty, to change its republican form, or to deprive it of its constitutional powers, would be void."

7. *Reid v. Covert,* 354 U.S. 1 (1957). Although only four justices subscribed to that opinion, the concurring and dissenting opinions did not question the main affirmations of constitutional supremacy in the plurality opinion, but only the application of the argument to the special circumstances of military courts martial for military dependents (since the Constitution does give explicit authority for Congress to "make rules for the government and regulation of the land and naval forces"). The opinion has been cited by the Supreme Court more than a hundred times since then, without any indication that the general affirmations in the plurality opinion are anything less than secure precedent. In *Boos v. Barry,* 485 U.S. 312 (1988), for example, *Reid* was invoked as authority for the holding that, notwithstanding a treaty on diplomatic courtesies, the First Amendment must supersede a law prohibiting picketing in front of foreign embassies in Washington.

8. *Reid v. Covert,* 354 U.S. 1 (1957) at 5–6, 14.

9. Ibid. at 16–18.

10. Justice Kennedy's recent concurring opinion in *Clinton v. New York* , 118 S. Ct. 2091 (1998) at 2109, put the point this way:

> In recent years, perhaps, we have come to think of liberty as defined by that word in the Fifth and Fourteenth Amendments and as illuminated by the other provisions of the Bill of Rights. The conception of liberty embraced by the Framers was not so confined. They used the principles of separation of powers and federalism to secure liberty in the fundamental political sense of the term, quite in addition to the idea of freedom from intrusive governmental acts. The idea and the promise were that when the people delegate some degree of control to a remote central authority, one branch of government ought not possess the power to shape their destiny without a sufficient check from the other two. In that vision, liberty demands limits on the ability of any one branch to influence basic political decisions.

11. Third *Restatement of the Foreign Relations Law of the United States,* § 111, Comment (i).

12. Ibid.

13. Quincy Wright, *The Control of American Foreign Relations* (Macmillan Co., 1922), pp. 95–126, treats many ramifications of

the underlying doctrine that the powers of constitutional organs of the United States cannot be delegated by treaty. Though he was eager to defend the constitutional propriety of American participation in the League of Nations, Wright was quite emphatic about the nondelegation principle: "[T]he treaty making power exercises legislative power which cannot be delegated" (p. 104). Even if the proposed recipient of the delegation were a quasi-judicial commission, the conclusion is the same: "A delegation of political power, that is legislative or treaty-making power, to such a body would be unconstitutional" (p. 125). Louis Henkin, one of the leading contemporary scholars, takes a far more ac-commodating view, arguing that delegations to international agencies can be seen as extensions of the general trend toward delegating legislative power to executive agencies: where "legis-lative" or "regulatory" powers are given to international agen-cies, they may be "properly seen as implementations of the origi-nal treaty establishing the organization and giving it 'regulatory powers' and, in consenting to that agreement, the Senate may be said to have consented in advance to any regulations authorized by that agreement." Henkin, *Foreign Affairs and the Constitution*, 2d ed. (Oxford University Press, 1996), p. 263.

14. 62d Cong., 1st Sess., S. Doc. 98, p. 6; *Congressional Record* 47: 3935; quoted by Wright, *Control*, p. 111. The argument seems to be overdrawn when applied to any and all delegations. In par-ticular, if the United States must retain total authority to deter-mine for itself in all respects what a treaty means, then there can be no international arbitration or adjudication of any kind—which no prominent jurist or commentator has ever contended. The traditional view was that international arbitration can inter-pret the external or international obligations of the United States, under a specific treaty or customary rule of international law, so long as the decision does not have direct effect in U.S. (domes-tic) law. U.S. authorities must then decide how (or perhaps, ulti-mately whether) to implement the decision of the tribunal. But the nondelegation argument has force if it means that delega-tion must be within reasonably close limits, even in relation to determining the external obligations of the United States—that is, its obligations as understood by other countries as a matter of international law.

15. Pitman B. Potter, "Inhibitions upon the Treaty-Making Power of the United States," 28 *American Journal of International*

Law, vol. 28 (1934), p. 456, reports the objections pressed by the American delegates (H. M. Robinson and Samuel Gompers) at the 1919 conference that drafted the constitution of the ILO. The first objection was that "[t]o permit a foreign body to conclude a treaty binding upon the United States would be equivalent to delegating the power of making treaties in the measure of the provisions of the treaty in question."

16. Among the few ILO conventions that have been ratified are those that deal directly with international commerce, as with the convention governing relations between masters and seamen in ocean shipping (October 24, 1936: 54 Stat. 1683, 1693, 1705). But, characteristically, the Clinton administration recently urged the Senate to ratify an ILO convention dealing with employment discrimination, which has no connection to international commerce, and would extend existing U.S. standards in that area to prohibit discrimination based on "social origin" and "political opinion." *BNA Employment Discrimination Report,* May 27, 1998, p. 682.

17. President Reagan's statement explaining those objections appears in *The Weekly Compilation of Presidential Documents* 887 (1982), p. 18.

18. *Carter v. Carter Coal,* 298 U.S. 238, 311 (1936). While the portion of that ruling dealing with federal power under the Commerce Clause has been largely superseded, the nondelegation argument continues to be treated respectfully. See, for example, *Loving v. United States,* 116 S. Ct. 1737, 1743–44 (1996).

19. The distinction does not rest simply on the presumption of some special sense of loyalty or civic spirit on the part of private American citizens. American citizens who take part in governmental undertakings may be subject to disclosure laws and ultimately to criminal sanctions for perjury, fraud, or misconduct in ways that would be unavailing against officials of international agencies or foreign diplomats, let alone against foreign governments.

20. Technically, one might distinguish two sorts of delegation issues here. Some treaties are regarded as self-executing, meaning that they operate directly in U.S. domestic law and can be enforced directly by U.S. courts as full equivalents of domestic legislation. The Warsaw Convention, setting limitations on tort recovery after international airline crashes, is a well-known, contemporary example: U.S. courts apply its terms as if the treaty

were an act of Congress. Most international treaties are not self-executing in this sense: they may impose obligations on the United States that other countries regard as legally binding, but subsequent legislation must still implement them and U.S. courts cannot directly enforce them. Delegation of "legislative power" is more objectionable in relation to self-executing treaties. It remains open to serious objections, however, even in the case of non-self-executing treaties. One might, more precisely, describe the delegation in such a case as involving a delegation of "treaty-making power" rather than "legislative power." But so long as treaties are regarded as imposing legal obligations—and even legal obligations of a purely "external" character remain, in some sense, legal obligations—the power to make such obligations cannot be delegated without limit. Suppose, in the extreme case, that Congress voted to say that the United States would be legally bound by any foreign commitment undertaken on its behalf by the government of Great Britain. Such a posture is by no means inconceivable: it was, in fact, the constitutional posture of Canada and Australia until 1931, decades after they achieved full self-government in domestic matters. Does the Constitution really place no limit on the authority of Congress—whether by treaty or otherwise—to put the United States into the position of a self-governing dominion of a foreign empire? Is the constitutional objection any less severe because the relevant empire flies under the blue and white flag of the United Nations rather than the red, white, and blue of the Union Jack?

21. See the objections to such features in the Gramm-Rudman legislation, requiring the president to implement the decisions of the comptroller general in *Bowsher v. Synar,* 478 U.S. 714 (1986). The Justice Department raised similar objections to proposed reservations to a treaty on the hunting of fur seals in the Bering Straits: when the Senate sought to attach a reservation requiring the president to direct U.S. representatives on an international commission to vote in a prescribed way, the Justice Department insisted that the president's responsibility "to take care that the laws be faithfully executed" means that the president alone can determine how treaties are to be implemented (though the Senate can attach understandings or reservations that specify what the treaty means). "Constitutionality of Proposed Conditions to Senate Consent to the Interim Convention on Conservation of North Pacific Fur Seals," 10 Op. O.L.C. 17 (1986).

NOTES TO PAGES 16–17

22. Wright, *Control*, pp. 119–20, notes constitutional objections to proposed reservations to the treaty establishing the League of Nations on the grounds that they might be regarded as restricting inherent responsibilities of the president as commander-in-chief. Today, the question may be whether the president can yield up his responsibility as commander-in-chief under international agreements setting up peace-keeping forces with U.S. participation under UN command.

23. Wright, *Control*, p. 118, notes that the United States refused to enter a treaty to establish an international prize court in 1909, a position that emphasized just this problem. As the U.S. delegation explained: "The decision of national courts cannot be annulled by foreign decisions in certain countries, such as the United States of America. Recourse to the Prize Court might have that effect of annulling a decision of the Supreme Court of the United States, a result incompatible with their Constitution."

24. The Inter-American Human Rights Court has been less active than the European Court on Human Rights, partly because it has been fully established for a much shorter period, but it now has jurisdiction (that is, states have submitted to its authority) in every country of Central and South America. Two distinguishing attributes of the Inter-American Court, compared with its European counterpart, are that it has developed a wider, formal procedure for the participation of private human rights advocates and has given itself the authority to issue advisory opinions. The Human Rights Commission of the Organization of American States, at which the United States does participate as a member of the OAS, also monitors compliance with the Inter-American Convention on Human Rights and in that capacity has reviewed several claims against the United States, such as complaints that U.S. abortion law inadequately protects "the right to life" (as defined in the convention) and that police officials in Philadelphia used excessive force against the radical sect "Move" in 1979. The commission became the first intergovernmental human rights body to find the United States in violation of international human rights norms (Case 9647, Inter-American C.H.R. 147, OEA/ser. L/V/11/71, doc. 9 rev. 1 (1987)), holding that the United States violated Articles I (right to life) and II (equality before the law) of the Inter-American Declaration on Human Rights in the sentencing to death and execution of two juvenile offenders. Though the commission asserted that its ruling was

legally binding, the case was not pursued to the Inter-American
Court of Human Rights, as it could have been if the United States
had ratified the full Inter-American Convention on Human
Rights. See Christina M. Cerna, "International Law and the Protection of Human Rights in the Inter-American System," *Houston
Journal of International Law,* vol. 19 (1997), p. 731, n. 60 (on challenge to U.S. abortion laws) and n. 63 (on the death penalty);
Martin Olz, "Non-Governmental Organizations in Regional Human Rights Systems," *Columbia Human Rights Law Review,* vol. 28
(Winter 1997), p. 307 (on distinctive provisions for participation
by NGOs).

25. Historic objections to sharing the jurisdiction of U.S.
courts with international tribunals are surveyed—and ostensibly
refuted—in Paul Marquardt, "Law without Borders: The Constitutionality of an International Criminal Court," *Columbia Journal
of Transnational Law,* vol. 33 (1995), p. 73. The position of the
Clinton administration is explained in the July 23, 1998, "Statement by the Ambassador at Large for War Crimes Issues and Head
of the U.S. delegation to the UN Diplomatic Conference on the
Establishment of a Permanent International Criminal Court before the Senate Foreign Relations Committee," (distributed by
Federal News Service). Wider objections are surveyed in the testimony to the same hearing by John R. Bolton, former assistant
secretary of state for international organizations. A notable feature of the proposed new "statute" for the International Criminal Court is that it would authorize the Court to initiate prosecutions even when national courts had already tried the defendant
and found him innocent or administered what international pros-
ecutors consider to be inadequate punishment. Thus, the statute
would provide the equivalent of appellate review of U.S. proceedings.

26. See, for example, James Chen, "Appointments with Disas-
ter: The Unconstitutionality of Binational Arbitral Review under
the U.S.-Canada Free Trade Agreement," *Washington & Lee Law
Review,* vol. 49 (1992), pp. 1455–99. The arguments are given
notice in *Coalition for Competitive Trade v. Clinton,* 128 F.3d 761
(D.C. Cir. 1997), which cited standing and other jurisdictional
barriers in declining to rule on the merits.

27. *New York v. United States,* 505 U.S. 144 (1992), at 168–69.

28. Ibid.

29. *Printz v. United States,* 117 S. Ct. 2365 (1997), at 2378.

30. To be sure, the Emoluments Clause does allow Congress to make exceptions: accepting foreign emoluments or titles is prohibited "without the consent of the Congress." That provision for exceptions seems to have been designed to accommodate minor diplomatic courtesies. That Congress was not being authorized to grant wholesale dispensations from the prohibition is suggested by the placement of this provision in Section 9, where all the other provisions deal not with grants of power but special restrictions on congressional power.

31. Thomas Jefferson, *Manual of Parliamentary Practice* (1797), sec. 52: "By the general power to make treaties, the Constitution must have intended to comprehend only those objects which are usually regulated by treaty and cannot be otherwise regulated."

32. *Geofroy v. Riggs*, 133 U.S. 258, 267 (1890). Similar statements, limiting the reach of the treaty power to "proper subjects" of international concern, appear in *Holmes v. Jennison*, 14 Pet. 540, 569 (1840); *Holden v. Joy*, 17 Wall. 211, 243 (1870); *Asakura v. City of Seattle*, 265 U.S. 332, 341 (1924), and other cases.

33. *Proceedings of the American Society of International Law*, vol. 23 (1929), pp. 194–96.

34. In this field of law, the Second *Restatement* was the first ever published (though it was published at the time when other restatements were in "second" editions).

35. Sec. 302, comment (c) and reporter's n. 2 (Second *Restatement*).

Chapter 3: The Expanding Reach of International Law

1. In a speech before the House of Representatives on February 9, 1943, Rep. Claire Booth Luce attacked the rhetoric of Vice President Henry Wallace in these terms: "Much of what [he] calls his global thinking is, no matter how you slice it, still Globaloney." And she seems to have been voicing an outlook already quite familiar. The inaugural issue of the *American Journal of International Law* carried an article that complained about American views of international law in this way: "Americans are prone to think that a nation with so many people, so many millions of money and so many ships of war must have always sound views on diplomacy; what is desirable for their comfort and the peace of their neighborhood seems to them international law."

NOTES TO PAGES 23–24

Albert Bushnell Hart, "American Ideals of International Relations," *American Journal of International Law,* vol.1 (1907), p. 635.

2. The most important of the reservations sought to pin down
the constitutional restrictions discussed in the previous chapter:
that Congress cannot delegate to an international body the power
to declare war, the power to appropriate money or impose tariffs, nor the power to control U.S. law on immigration or other
matters. For the precise wording of the reservations and the text
of committee reports explaining their constitutional justifications,
see Henry Cabot Lodge, *The Senate and the League of Nations*
(Scribners, 1925), chap. 10, especially pp. 182–85.

3. At one point during the Philadelphia Convention, James
Wilson protested against a proposal to give Congress power to
"define" (as well as to "punish") "offenses against the law of nations" on the grounds that "the law of nations . . . depended on
the authority of all the Civilized Nations of the World," so unilateral American action here would "have a look of arrogance that
would make us ridiculous." Wilson's argument was voted down,
however. The counterargument by Gouverneur Morris was suc-
cinct: "The word define is proper when applied to offences in
this case; the law [of nations] being often too vague and defi-
cient to be a rule." Max Farrand, ed., *Records of the Federal Convention,* vol. 2, p. 615 (debate on September 14) (Yale University
Press, 1911, reprinted 1966). No one argued, however, that traditional notions regarding the law of nations should be altogether
ignored.

4. Although the United States reserved to itself the power to
"define" those "offenses"—at least for actions in U.S. courts—
the clause does reflect an acknowledgment that the United States
had some obligation to act against such international offenses
(principally piracy and depredations against ambassadors). Congress could prohibit the same conduct, presumably without calling it an "offense against the law of nations," but the Constitution presumes that the United States will want to present itself as
a respectable supporter of the "law of nations."

5. "The law of nations is the law of sovereigns. . . . [A]s the
law of nature, in other words, as the will of nature's God, it is
indispensably binding upon the people, in whom the sovereign
power resides; and who are, consequently, under the most sa-
cred obligations to exercise that power . . . in a manner agree-

able to those rules and maxims which the law of nature prescribes to every state, for the happiness of each and for the happiness of all." Wilson, "Lectures on Law" (lecture 4), in Robert G. McCloskey, ed., *The Works of James Wilson*, vol. 1 (Harvard University Press, 1967), p. 153.

6. Madison, *Examination of the British Doctrine Which Subjects to Capture a Neutral Trade Not Open in Time of Peace* (originally published in London in 1806; reprinted in Gaillard Hunt, ed., *The Writings of James Madison*, vol. 7 (G.P. Putnam's Sons, 1908), pp. 204–375).

7. Here, for example, is the characterization offered by Theodore D. Woolsey, *Introduction to International Law* (4th ed., Scribner, Armstrong & Co., 1876):

> [W]e define international law to be the aggregate of the rules which Christian states acknowledge with each other. . . . [T]he definition cannot justly be widened to include the law which governs Christian states in their intercourse with savage or half-civilized tribes; or even with nations on a higher level, but lying outside their forms of civilization. In general, towards such nations they have acted on the principle that there is no common bond of obligation between them. . . . Especially toward savage tribes they have often acted with flagrant selfishness, as if they feared no retribution and were beyond the reach of public opinion (§ 5, pp. 19–20).

8. James Kent, "Lecture 1," *Commentaries on American Law*, vol. 1, 14th ed., (Little, Brown, 1896) (with notes by Oliver Wendell Holmes, updated by J. M. Gould), p. 19. Originally published in 1826, Kent's classic work was lovingly annotated and updated by scholars throughout the nineteenth century. The first of Kent's three volumes starts with an overview of the "law of nations" before turning to "Government and Constitutional Jurisprudence of the United States"—with the implication that the law of nations establishes the most general principles under which the United States claims the legal authority to assert its own constitution and law for its own territory. Kent describes that as a "branch of jurisprudence" that is "necessary to lawyers and statesmen" but also "highly ornamental to every scholar who wishes to be adorned with the accomplishments of various learning" (p. 19).

9. Henry Wheaton, *Elements of International Law* (originally published in 1836; citations from 8th ed., Richard H. Dana, ed., Little, Brown, 1866), part 1, § 15, ¶ 2, p. 24: "[T]hough one or two treaties varying from the general usage and custom of nations cannot alter the international law, yet an almost perpetual succession of treaties, establishing a particular rule, will go far toward proving what that law is on a disputed point." The resistance to reformulations by treaty is implied in Wheaton's definition, which emphasizes the natural law derivation: "International law, as understood among civilized nations, may be defined as consisting of those *rules of conduct which reason deduces,* as consonant to justice, *from the nature of the society existing among independent nations*" (emphasis added) (part 1, § 14), p. 23. As Wheaton observes, the term *international law* came to be preferred to the older term precisely as a way of emphasizing that its subject matter is the relations between sovereign states, rather than shared or parallel legal traditions within various countries (as *the law of nations* might, in some contexts, seem to suggest) (part 1, § 12, ¶ 4, p. 20).

10. Kent, "Lecture 1," *Commentaries on American Law,* pp. 2–3.

11. Emmerich de Vattel, *The Law of Nations* (Fenwick, tr., Carnegie, 1916). Vattel's work was so frequently cited that some scholars speculate it was the literary source for Jefferson's phrase "the pursuit of happiness." Forrest McDonald, *Novus Ordo Seculorum: The Intellectual Origins of the Constitution* (University Press of Kansas, 1985), pp. ix–x.

12. Vattel, bk. 2, chap. 4, § 54 and § 55. Even in the nineteenth century, however, when the Supreme Court still cited Vattel as an authoritative guide, the United States felt free to express concern about, and even condemnation of, what would now be called human rights abuses. In the 1840s, for example, the United States broke off diplomatic relations with the Papal States to protest repression of Protestant churches in the Pope's temporal dominions. Vattel's strictures seem to have been interpreted as a prohibition on direct or coercive intervention. But nothing can require the United States to maintain diplomatic courtesies or even full trade relations (let alone to give foreign aid) to regimes of which it disapproves.

13. Kent, "Lecture 2," *Commentaries on American Law,* p. 21.

Like Vattel (and like the Declaration of Independence), Kent starts by positing the equality of independent states and treats the principle of sovereignty as "a necessary consequence of this equality."

14. H. W. Halleck, *International Law or Rules Regulating the Intercourse of States in Peace and War* (D. Van Nostrand, 1861), chap. 2, § 8, p. 86: the subtitle offers a fair indication of Halleck's view of the proper subject matter of "international law." And Halleck was not a fussy academic. He was a life-long army officer who wrote a major manual on infantry tactics before taking up international law. General William T. Sherman pronounced Halleck a "man of great capacity," and Sherman had reason to know: Halleck was commander of Union forces in the Western District in the first years of the Civil War, where he directed the initial ventures of Grant and Sherman and then, as Army chief of staff after 1863, helped coordinate their victorious campaigns in the East. Yet Halleck also commissioned the first army manual on the "laws of war." Sherman invoked it to justify his order that civilians be evacuated from Atlanta. *Memoirs of W. T. Sherman* (Library of America, 1990), pp. 274, 602.

15. Of course, victors in war did sometimes impose such restrictions, though they often then failed to enforce them. The point here is simply that it was still quite possible to argue that such restrictions, even if imposed by treaty, were actually contrary to the principles of international law, because international law was thought to be based on principles, and the core principle was thought to be respect for the sovereign rights of independent states.

16. See T. E. Holland, *Lectures on International Law* (Thomas Alfred Walker and Wyndham Legh Walker, eds., Sweet & Maxwell, Ltd., 1933), p. 176, reporting the view of Bluntschli and other nineteenth-century European legal scholars that treaties for "immoral objects" must be void—and citing "surrender of independence" as one of the examples offered by such scholars.

17. Actually, the achievement was disguised or perhaps not quite so dramatic as it is sometimes seen. The opening provisions of the Declaration of Paris purported to recognize an existing fact: "Privateering is, and remains abolished." Neither Britain nor France had resorted to the practice during the Crimean War (the peace treaty for which was negotiated at the same Congress of Paris that produced the Declaration on Maritime Law in

Time of War). So privateering, though still asserted by British and French jurists on the eve of the peace conference, had not actually been practiced by a major power since the Napoleonic Wars, some forty years before. Of the forty-two countries that acceded to the declaration (all in Europe, apart from a handful in Latin America), none had recently relied on privateering, and most had never done so. The United States refused to accede to the Declaration on the grounds that it did not go far enough to protect the private property of citizens from belligerent powers (whose property would still be subject to capture by authorized naval forces under the terms of the declaration). But notwithstanding its failure to join the new international consensus, the United States did not itself resort to privateering, even in its war with Spain in 1898, though Spain was also a nonadherent to the Declaration of Paris. Useful background is provided in Janice E. Thomson, *Mercenaries, Pirates, and Sovereigns* (Princeton University Press, 1994), pp. 69–75.

18. Paul S. Reinsch, "International Unions and Their Administration," *American Journal of International Law*, vol. 1 (1907), p. 579.

19. Frederick Sherwood Dunn, "International Legislation," *Political Science Quarterly*, vol. 42 (1926), p. 571, noted that this "phenomenon" had already "enjoyed a vigorous and lusty growth for more than half a century" but was "not yet admitted into the accepted classification and terminology of . . . the science of international jurisprudence" and was "all but ignored in the standard treatises on international law." He cited only one use of the term (and that "in a qualified manner") from the nineteenth century and several from the early twentieth century that reinforce his point that the term is not established in scholarly or official usage. He provided a list of over fifty "legislative treaties," most of which, however, reflected agreements in Europe on rights of passage, established in successive treaties by "the Great Powers" of Europe.

20. *The Federalist* No. 20 (Clinton Rossiter, ed., Mentor, NAL Penguin, 1961, p. 138).

21. *Convention on Biological Diversity*, 31 I.L.M. 818 (1992); *Statement of Principles for a Global Consensus on the Management, Conservation and Sustainable Development of All Types of Forests*, 31 I.L.M. 881 (1992); *Convention on the Elimination of All Forms of Discrimination against Women*, 19 I.L.M. 33 (1980); *Convention on the Rights of*

the Child, 28 I.L.M. 1448 (1989); *Declaration on the Rights of Persons Belonging to National, Ethnic, Religious and Linguistic Minorities* (1992); *General Assembly Resolution on the International Decade of the World's Indigenous People* (A/RES/48/163, Dec. 21, 1993) (among other things, "[w]elcoming the report of the United Nations Conference on Environment and Development, in which the vital role of indigenous people and their communities in the interrelationship between the natural environment and its sustainable development is recognized, including their holistic traditional scientific knowledge of their lands, natural resources and environment"); Declaration on the Rights of Indigenous Peoples (draft approved by Res. 1994/45 of the Subcommission on Prevention of Discrimination and Protection of Minorities, UN High Commissioner for Human Rights, 36th meeting, August 26, 1994).

22. In 1987, for example, the UN Commission on Human Rights passed a resolution calling upon Chile to reorganize its internal police force, although matters of internal public administration have traditionally been considered a leading example of "domestic concerns." International jurists have argued that such resolutions do not violate the "essentially domestic" exclusion because, not being directly binding, they are not "interventions." Kamminga, *Interstate Accountability* (University of Pennsylvania Press, 1992), p. 96. It is not clear what, short of dispatching troops, does count as intervention—and it is still less clear whether, in case troops were dispatched, anything could be excluded from their control as touching matters "essentially within the domestic jurisdiction" of the "host" state. In the aftermath of the Gulf War, UN resolutions did seek to impose strict controls on Iraqi weapons production, backed by regular UN inspections of suspected production sites within Iraq. The Security Council ignored protests from the Iraqis that this violated their sovereignty and their domestic jurisdiction. Whether that episode has established an important precedent is uncertain, however, since the UN so rarely can exercise the authority of a victorious military force and has had great difficulty mustering the will to see through its own resolutions, even in this case. "Domestic jurisdiction" thus seems to be protected by the feebleness of the UN, rather than by any definite juridical boundary.

23. So, for example, Rhoads, *Incomparable Worth,* pp. 137–38, notes that the European Commission has found it easier to bring suits against Britain because the British legal system provides more

transparency, allowing officials in Brussels to determine more reliably what actual legal practice is in the United Kingdom.

24. Louis Henkin maintained, some twenty years ago, that "almost all nations observe almost all principles of international law and almost all of their obligations all the time." *How Nations Behave*, 2d ed. (Columbia University Press, 1979), p. 47. The point has been emphasized with more recent examples by Abram Chayes and Antonia Handler Chayes, "On Compliance," *International Organization,* vol.47 (1993), p. 1755, and their subsequent book, *The New Sovereignty: Compliance with International Regulatory Agreements* (Harvard University Press, 1995). The Chayes claim that nations often fail to comply with their international commitments because they lack the resources or internal capacities to do so but rarely respond to complaints about noncompliance with open defiance, because they are eager to remain in "good standing" with the international community. They try to prove the argument by citing various examples, drawn from different fields of contemporary international regulation.

Abram Chayes had previously written major articles in the 1970s and 1980s defending "public law litigation" in U.S. courts (where federal judges preside over continuing institutional reform in complex, multiparty suits, as in school desegregation and prison reform). Chayes seems to view international cooperation in the same light as bargaining among parties in those complex domestic cases, where judges lack the resources to do effective monitoring or direction and depend largely on side bargaining by the various parties. What the analogy suggests (and what the Chayes survey seems to confirm) is that compliance is to a large extent a function of the effort that concerned countries invest in trying to "jawbone" cheaters or laggards into fuller compliance. But that means that compliance will appear to be satisfactory when no country thinks it worthwhile to invest great effort in monitoring compliance—which is undoubtedly a frequent situation, given distracting and competing diplomatic agendas. Particularly where one country's action has no direct effects on another (as in human rights agreements), there is a very low level of enforcement. Even then, cases of open defiance exist. Evidently relying on low to nonexistent enforcement, North Korea actually signed the covenant on Civil and Political Rights. When criticized by the UN's Human Rights Committee (by vote of 13–9–2) for failure to adhere to its terms, North Korea simply announced that it would repudiate the covenant (Kyodo News International Inc., Sept. 1, 1997). Behind the scenes, then, noncompliant countries may threaten to stomp out of the game in that way and reveal the empty pretensions of a "cooperation" regime. There is no actual judge in the background, as in domestic bargaining in institutional reform litigation. Thus, demands for strict compliance are not likely to be very strenuous—least of all from those who wish to uphold the vision that "international cooperation" is reliable and improving.

If it were really true that almost all countries conscientiously comply with almost all international standards almost all of the time, that fact would demonstrate that reliable enforcement authority is not really necessary in human affairs, because expressions of displeasure by others are enough to hold almost all people to their obligations almost all of the time. For some reason, enthusiasts of international cooperation do not seem inclined to apply such a highly optimistic, libertarian outlook to domestic affairs.

25. Pierre-Marie Dupuy, "Soft Law and the International Law of the Environment," *Michigan Journal of International Law*, vol. 12 (1991), p. 420, stresses two factors in the growth of soft law. First, the "existence and development of a ramified network of permanent institutions . . . [in which the] 'UN family' of organizations plays the leading role" and connected with that, "the increasingly important function of nongovernmental organizations . . . assuring . . . a dynamic relation between inter-State diplomacy and international public opinion." And second, "the arrival of underdeveloped countries on the international stage" that, "having the weight of the majority without the power of the elder countries, have speculated on the utilization of 'soft' instruments, such as resolutions and recommendations of international bodies, with a view toward modifying a number of the main rules and principles of the international legal order."

26. Report of the Commission on Global Governance, *Our Global Neighborhood* (Oxford University Press, 1995), pp. 70–71.

Chapter 4: The Real Threats from "Global Governance"

1. Earlier generations might have questioned the constitutional validity of such arrangements. See Bruce Ackerman and

David Golove, "Is NAFTA Constitutional?" *Harvard Law Review,* vol. 95 (1995), p. 799.

2. *B. Altman & Co. v. U.S.,* 224 U.S. 583 (1912), treating as equivalent to a treaty an executive agreement on reciprocal tariff reductions, negotiated under authorization of general tariff legislation.

3. *U.S. v. Belmont,* 301 U.S. 324 (1937), approving transfer to the Soviet Union from a New York bank of assets belonging to Russian nationals, pursuant to executive agreement, without congressional authorization and in disregard of contrary New York State policy.

4. Henry Steiner, *Transnational Legal Problems,* 4th ed. (Foundation Press, 1994), p. 561.

5. 1 U.S.C. § 112b (originally enacted in the early 1970s).

6. Detlev Vagts, "International Agreements, the Senate, and the Constitution," *Columbia Journal of Transnational Law,* vol. 36 (1997), p. 154.

7. Louis Henkin, *Foreign Affairs and the Constitution,* 2d ed. (Oxford University Press, 1996), pp. 254–55n.:

> Early in the twentieth century, Congress concluded that it can exercise its powers effectively only through administrative agencies and U.S. constitutional jurisprudence accommodated to that "fourth branch" of government. At the end of the twentieth century, the political branches have found that they can achieve effective governance only through international agencies. Is there any reason why the Constitution cannot accommodate to that development?

8. See, most notably, Theodore Lowi, *The End of Liberalism,* 2d ed. (Norton, 1979), and David Schoenbrod, *Power without Responsibility: How Congress Abuses the People through Delegation* (Yale University Press, 1993).

9. Justice Rehnquist mounted a full-dress defense of the doctrine (though in dissent) in *Industrial Union Dept., AFL-CIO v. American Petroleum Institute,* 448 U.S. 607 (1980) at 672–76. That opinion has been cited quite respectfully in a number of subsequent opinions (for example, by Souter in *Weiss v. United States,* 510 U.S. 163 (1994). Most recently, the Court struck down the line-item veto (in *Clinton v. New York,* 118 S. Ct. 2091 (1998)), for allowing the president to repeal provisions of budget law without

a separate vote by Congress and thereby to evade the legislative process set out in Article I, Section 7. As the dissent by Justice Breyer points out, however, the argument is not entirely convincing in these terms: when the president exercises the line-item veto, his action need not be seen as "repealing" a budget law or as "making" a new budget law but simply as implementing the discretion accorded to him by the line-item veto law. Thus, the majority's real objection seems to be that the veto law delegated excessive discretion—amounting to a delegation of legislative authority—to the president. In fact, Marci Hamilton and David Schoenbrod argued that position very cogently in an amicus brief, citing several Supreme Court decisions of the past two decades that can be understood as implicit endorsements of the nondelegation doctrine. And Justice Kennedy's concurring opinion in *Clinton*, while not invoking the nondelegation doctrine by name, does offer a quite eloquent and sophisticated statement of the underlying rationale for the doctrine: "The Constitution's structure requires a stability which transcends the convenience of the moment. . . . Abdication of responsibility is not part of the constitutional design" (pp. 2198–99).

10. "Discretion and Legitimacy in International Regulation," *Harvard Law Review,* vol. 107 (1994), p. 1099.

11. See, for example, Peter Haas, "Do Regimes Matter? Epistemic Communities and Mediterranean Pollution Control," *International Organization,* vol. 43 (1989), pp. 401–2. For an instance in the human rights field, note the Convention on the Rights of the Child, negotiated during the 1980s—the era of the Reagan administration: despite the contrary public commitments of the Reagan administration, no American representative at UN drafting sessions raised any questions about the evident preference of this text for state-directed and state-financed child welfare policies (at least so far as appears from the minutes of the official drafting sessions). No effort seems to have been made to coordinate actual Reagan administration policies with the negotiating postures of the delegations participating in the drafting of that convention.

12. In 1991, for example, the UN Development Programme (UNDP) tried to develop indexes to measure human freedom. Of the twenty countries that ranked lowest on that index—that is, the twenty UN member states with the lowest scores for protection of human freedom, fully half had already ratified the In-

ternational Covenant on Civil and Political Rights (including Iraq, Libya, Syria, Zaire, Vietnam, North Korea, Bulgaria, Romania, and the then-USSR). The list (without reference to ICCPR ratification) appears in UNDP, *Human Development Report, 1991* (Oxford University Press, 1991), p. 20. The publication of that index created such a storm that the UNDP decided not to continue it. The UNDP did forge ahead, however, with a separate index of human development (corresponding to basic elements of economic welfare). Of the ten states scoring lowest on that index in 1996, half had already ratified the Covenant on Economic and Social Rights (Niger, Somalia, Mali, Afghanistan, and Burundi). See UNDP, *Human Development Report, 1996* (Oxford University Press, 1996), pp. 135–37 (again without reference to ICESR ratifications—which I have cross-referenced from other UN sources).

13. Richard Benedick, *Ozone Diplomacy, New Directions in Safeguarding the Planet* (Harvard University Press, 1991), pp. 148–58, 188–89, 196.

14. One of the most serious concerns is that vaccines against killing diseases must be refrigerated to be effective, and the CFC ban thus seems to have threatened public health efforts in poor countries. Gary Stix, "Keeping Vaccines Cold," *Scientific American,* February 1996, pp. 14–16.

Poor countries have done even more grotesque things at the prompting of Western environmentalists. In the mid-1980s, the government of Zimbabwe killed over fifty people for poaching on elephant reserves. The government used an attack helicopter, purchased with donated funds (and the complete foreknowledge) of the Worldwide Fund for Nature. The same organization even donated funds for a project that recruited British and South African mercenaries to train antipoacher hit squads. Government forces in Kenya then killed several dozen poachers with a new shoot-on-sight policy, and the policy was applauded by the African Wildlife Foundation, which is based in the United States. The fundraising and rhetorical imperatives of Western environmentalists then led to a successful campaign for an international ban on trade in rhino and elephant tusks (ivory), even though officials in several African countries thought conservation would be better encouraged by allowing some trade, thereby giving local people some incentive to protect wildlife. See Raymond Bonner, *At the Hand of Man* (Knopf, 1993), especially pp. 18, 78, 126–27, 155–57.

15. Convention on the Control of Transboundary Movements of Hazardous Wastes and Their Disposal (completed March 22, 1989, entered into force May 5, 1992), reprinted in 28 I.L.M. 657.

16. At a recent meeting of the parties to the Basel Convention, the developed countries rejected applications from Israel and other reasonably developed countries to join their ranks. "Parties to Basel Convention Adopt Two-List System for Waste Export," *BNA International Environment,* March 4, 1998, p. 185. That decision strongly suggests that what is presented as a protective measure for poor countries is, in practice, an international cartel that excludes willing participants from certain markets. But the decision was strongly supported by Greenpeace International, taking the same position in this as major European governments. Greenpeace International draws the bulk of its funding from countries in northern Europe.

17. Completed March 3, 1973, entered into force July 1, 1975, 27 U.S.T. 1087, 993 U.N.T.S. 243.

18. Bonner, *At the Hand of Man,* describes the perverse incentives that the ban on ivory trade has had on efforts at rhino and elephant conservation in Africa and traces the support of Western environmentalists for that destructive policy to the imperatives of fundraising in Western countries.

19. Thus, international NGOs have become "an integral part of the negotiating process" in the making of new environmental agreements. Elin Enge and Runar Malkenes, "Non-Governmental Organizations at UNCED," *Green Globe Yearbook of International Cooperation on Environment and Development* (Oxford University Press, 1993), p. 25. Another study notes that NGO activists have "changed the face of international environmental law." David Tolbert, "Global Climate Change and the Role of International NGOs," in Robin Churchill and David Freestone, eds., *International Law and Global Climate Change* (Graham and Trotman, 1992), p. 108. Recent international treaties, in fact, make explicit provision for the participation of NGOs. The 1987 Montreal Protocol on Substances That Deplete the Ozone Layer started the trend with a stipulation that "any body . . . whether governmental or non-governmental, qualified in fields relating to the protection of the ozone layer, which has informed the secretariat of its wish to be represented at a meeting of the parties as an observer, may be admitted unless at least one-third of the Parties present ob-

ject," Art. 11, reprinted in 26 I.L.M. at 1558. Similar language appears in the 1992 Framework Convention on Climate Change, where the phrase "qualified in fields relating to" is softened to "qualified in matters covered by the Convention" (31 I.L.M. at 862). Similar patterns have developed in the field of human rights and labor rights (in the latter of which, participation by labor and employer groups has been standard procedure from the origins of the ILO under the League of Nations).

20. Report of the Commission on Global Governance, *Our Global Neighborhood* (Oxford University Press, 1995), pp. 254–55.

21. The parallels have been drawn at length by a sympathetic observer in Kal Raustalia, "The 'Participatory Revolution' in International Environmental Law," *Harvard Environmental Law Review*, vol. 21 (1997), p. 537, stressing the way in which NGO participation in international forums parallels the expanded standing given to environmental advocates in U.S. administrative law during the 1970s:

> As under the notice and comment requirements of the APA, NGOs are now often given access to documents and proposed treaty text. These working drafts of documents and treaty texts present in essence the subject of the "rule-making" (i.e., notice). In addition to the pervasive and informal "corridor lobbying" (i.e., comment), NGOs are allowed to speak from the floor with simultaneous translation, and may circulate draft texts of their own design. Private organizations are also allowed to distribute their own materials and commentaries. NGO draft documents are often widely relied upon by states and have influenced the evolution and creation of several environmental treaties. ... Like procedural changes in U.S. law, these procedural changes in international law allow greater transparency, access and interaction between stakeholders and rulemakers. In the former, the overarching goal was the incorporation of a wide array of under-represented public interests into an increasingly complex policy process. A similar guiding principle is apparent in the latter. ... As international environmental law has expanded its substantive ambit in significant ways, it has concurrently expanded access and participation by private actors, both regulated parties and beneficiaries of regulation. In doing so, the international community has traveled a path taken by American administrative law many years earlier.

22. For documentation of that pattern in an earlier phase and outside the field of contemporary environmental regulation, see David Strang and Patricia Mei Yin Chang, "The International Labor Organization and the Welfare State: Institutional Effects on National Welfare Spending, 1960–1980," *International Organization,* vol. 47 (Spring 1993), p. 235.

23. The Convention on the Rights of the Child is reprinted in 28 I.L.M. 1448 (1989). It includes: "[T]he right of every child to a standard of living adequate for the child's physical, mental, spiritual, moral and social development" and to that end, the right to have the state "provide material assistance and support programs" (Art. 27). The convention also includes the right to "education . . . directed to the development of the child's personality, talents and mental and physical abilities to their fullest potential and . . . development of respect for the child's . . . own cultural identity, language and values . . . in the spirit of understanding, peace, tolerance, equality of the sexes, and . . . respect for the natural environment" (Art. 29). Along with the right to a politically correct education, the child also "shall have . . . freedom to seek, receive, and impart information of all kinds . . . in print, in the form of art or through any other media of the child's choice" (Art. 13). And "[n]o child shall be subject to arbitrary . . . interference with his or her privacy . . . or correspondence" (Art. 16). And there must be recognition for "the rights of the child to freedom of association" (Art. 15). States must also "develop preventive health care . . . and family planning education and services" (Art. 24, 2(f)).

The Convention on the Elimination of All Forms of Discrimination against Women is reprinted in 19 I.L.M. 33 (1989). It includes an admonition to governments to "ensure to women, on equal terms with men, the right . . . to participate in the formulation of government policy . . . and perform all public functions at all levels of government" (Art. 7). The convention directs governments to ensure "the elimination of any stereotyped concept of the roles of men and women at all levels and in all forms of education . . . by the revision of textbooks and school programmes" (Art. 10). The convention also directs governments to "prohibit . . . [employment] dismissal on the basis of marital status" and admonishes them to "introduce maternity leave with pay" and "necessary social services" (Art. 11). It also demands "access to adequate health care, including . . . services for family planning."

24. Characteristically, while the general provisions of the treaty were submitted to the Senate, the nomination of specific U.S. sites (for coverage under the treaty) was made by the executive without congressional participation. The operating guidelines for the treaty—including a provision calling for controlled buffer zones around actual sites—were established by the World Heritage Committee and not even subject to U.S. acceptance by executive agreement. The committee operates under the sponsorship of UNESCO (which provides the majority of its funding), and the United States continued to cooperate in the activities of the committee, even though it had already withdrawn from UNESCO in protest against the political abuses of that UN agency.

25. For sampling of local press reaction, the original appeal to the World Heritage Committee by environmental advocates, and other key documents, see *Sovereignty over Public Lands: Hearings on H.R. 3752*, U.S. House of Representatives, Committee on Resources (104th Cong., 2d Sess.), September 12, 1996 (Serial No. 104-98), pp. 130–68 and pp. 43–44 (special interest in UN black helicopters by local representative).

26. The chairman of the World Heritage Committee at the time was Dr. Adul Wichiencharoen of Thailand, who led the delegation to Yellowstone, accompanied by Dr. Bernd von Droste of Germany. When the inspection was authorized, the World Heritage Committee included delegates from Brazil, China, Colombia, Cyprus, France, Germany, Indonesia, Italy, Japan, Lebanon, Mexico, Niger, Oman, Peru, the Philippines, Senegal, Spain, Thailand, and the United States. When the committee voted (at its Berlin meeting in December 1996) to place Yellowstone Park on its "in danger" list, the committee included delegates from Australia, Benin, Brazil, Canada, China, Cuba, Cyprus, Ecuador, France, Germany, Italy, Japan, Lebanon, Malta, Mexico, Morocco, Niger, the Philippines, Spain, and the United States. Delegates are nominated by member states and elected for two-year terms at the annual meeting of the parties to the World Heritage Convention. Minutes of the Berlin meeting at which Yellowstone was condemned (reportedly at the instigation of the U.S. assistant secretary of the Interior) are available on the UNESCO website at: http://www.unesco.org/whc/nwhc/pages/doc/main.htm.

Chapter 5: The Perils of Soft Law

1. U.S. Reservations and Understandings to the Genocide Convention are reprinted in 28 I.L.M. 782 (1989). For an extended analysis of the RUD package adopted then and in subsequent Senate ratifications of other human rights conventions, see David P. Stewart, "The Significance of Reservations, Understandings, and Declarations," *DePaul Law Review,* vol. 42 (1993), p. 1183.

2. Notably, Article III (c) defines as "acts . . . punishable" under the convention even "public incitement to commit genocide." Individual perpetrators are supposed to be subject to international criminal trial for that crime (Art. VI), including even those who merely have an undefined, III(d) "complicity in genocide" or are involved in an unsuccessful (b) "conspiracy" or (d) "attempt" to commit genocide. Such provisions might seem to pose only a small exception to free speech or due process guarantees—until one considers the way the convention actually defines *genocide.* Article II defines it to include "acts (b) [c]ausing . . . mental harm to members of the group; (c) . . . inflicting . . . conditions of life calculated to bring about . . . destruction . . . in part; (d) [i]mposing measures intended to prevent births within the group; (e) [f]orcibly transferring children of the group to another group." It might seem an absurd stretch for critics to invoke such provisions against, say, capital punishment or other crime-control measures that are disproportionately applied to members of minority groups. It might seem equally far-fetched to provide those provisions. Or those provisions may apply to allegedly inadequate gun-control or security measures in public housing or to inadequate drug-control or AIDS-prevention programs. So, also, those provisions may apply to limitations on welfare payments for additional children or court-ordered birth control implants or child removal in cases where drug addicts might be a danger to their own children. Yet the term *genocide* has already, in fact, been thrown around by critics of various policies affecting racial and ethnic minorities in inner cities—who do have shorter life expectancies and much higher death rates in certain age categories. If it seems unlikely that the Genocide Convention could be successfully invoked in relation to policy debates on such matters, one should consider whether it is in any way

more likely that actual mass murder will be restrained by a paper commitment to refrain from genocide. If the convention is not about making extreme rhetoric available for controversial policies of basically civilized regimes, what is it really about? Would there really be any doubt about the position of the U.S. government on mass murder, if it had not ratified the Genocide Convention?

3. International Covenant on Civil and Political Rights, 999 U.N.T.S. 171 (1966); Convention against Torture and Other Cruel, Inhuman or Degrading Treatment or Punishment, reprinted in 23 I.L.M. 1027; International Convention on the Elimination of All Forms of Racial Discrimination, 660 U.N.T.S. 195 (1966).

4. "[I]n England . . . the law of nations (wherever any question arises which is properly the object of its jurisdiction) is here adopted in its full extent by the common law and is held to be a part of the law of the land." William Blackstone, *Commentaries on the Laws of England*, bk. 4, chap. 5, ¶ 3, (facsimile of the first edition of 1765–1969, University of Chicago Press, 1979), vol. 4, p. 67.

5. James Kent, "Lecture 1," *Commentaries on American Law*, vol. 1, 14th ed. (Little, Brown, 1896) (with notes by Oliver Wendell Holmes, updated by J.M. Gould), p. 1, note (a).

6. *Paquete Habana*, 275 U.S. 677 (1900). The decision arose, however, in a case where the Supreme Court was acting as a prize court, pursuant to direct authorization from Congress, to determine the legality of seizures by the U.S. Navy in wartime (after the president had already announced that the Navy would follow international law in the war with Spain). The Court was not simply applying customary international law then but implementing a statute and an executive policy that expressly authorized it to do so in a very special setting.

7. To take two of the most important examples, sovereign immunity—the doctrine limiting the authority of a court in one country from entertaining a suit against the sovereign authority in another country—has been codified in federal statute since 1976 (Foreign Sovereign Immunities Act, 28 U.S.C. §§ 1330, 1602–11), and U.S. courts must follow that statute, rather than consult customary law principles. Similarly, questions about diplomatic immunity have been codified since 1961 in a formal treaty to

which the United States is a party (Vienna Convention on Diplomatic Relations, 23 U.S.T. 3227) obviating any need to consider customary international law in that area either.

8. *Erie R.R. v. Tompkins*, 304 U.S. 64 (1938).

9. 630 F.2d 876 (2d Cir., 1980).

10. Now at 28 U.S.C. § 1350, the Alien Tort Act was originally enacted as a provision of the Judiciary Act of 1789, § 9(b), 1 Stat. 73, 77. It seems to have been invoked by federal courts only once in the eighteenth century (in *Bolchos v. Darrel*, 3 Cas. 810 [D.S.C. 1795], Case No. 1,607) and then not at all until 1961 (in *Adra v. Clift*, 195 F. Supp. 857 [D. Md.]).

11. It has, since then, become standard practice for claims about customary international law to enter federal courts with an academic chaperone of expert testimony on the contemporary content of that law—which is otherwise so hard for judges to pin down. Richard Lillich, "The Growing Importance of Contemporary International Human Rights Law," *Georgia Journal of International and Comparative Law*, vol. 25 (1995–1996), p. 1, refers to "the ubiquitous . . . 'Affidavit of International Law Scholars' that has become the norm in recent human rights cases."

12. "Transnational Public Law Litigation," *Yale Law Journal*, vol. 100 (1991), p. 2366.

13. See, for example, *Kadic v. Karadzic*, 70 F.3d 232 (2d Cir., 1995); *Xuncas v. Gramajo*, 866 F. Supp. 162 (D. Mass. 1995); *Fernandez v. Wilkinson*, 505 F. Supp. 787 (D. Kan. 1980); *Republic of Philippines v. Marcos*, 806 F.2d 344 (2d Cir., 1986). An exception to the pattern is the D.C. Circuit ruling rejecting jurisdiction for such a suit under the ATS in *Tel-Oren v. Libyan Arab Republic*, 726 F.2d 774 (D.C. Cir., 1984), which includes a notable opinion by Judge Bork.

14. Pt. 7, chap. 1, §§ 701–703.

15. See, most notably, Curtis A. Bradley and Jack L. Goldsmith, "Customary International Law as Federal Common Law: A Critique of the Modern Position," *Harvard Law Review*, vol. 110 (February 1997), p. 815. A subsequent article by the same authors, "The Current Illegitimacy of International Human Rights Litigation," *Fordham Law Review*, vol. 66 (November 1997), p. 319, defends the argument against critics, of whom there are many, whereas (to judge from the extensive notations) few scholars as yet endorse that "critique."

16. The *Restatement*, itself, claims that its list of human rights norms already in customary international law "is not necessarily complete and is not closed: human rights not listed in this section may have achieved the status of customary law and some rights might achieve that status in the future" (§ 702, comment [a]). Less than a decade later, Louis Henkin, the chief reporter for the *Restatement*, declared in a public speech that "if he were drafting Section 702 today he would include as customary international law rights the right to property and freedom from gender discrimination, plus the right to personal autonomy and the right to live in a democratic society." Reported by Lillich, "The Growing Importance of Customary International Human Rights Law," p. 7, n. 43. Curiously, when the UN's Human Rights Committee published its own list in 1994, it did not include a single one of the new rights that Henkin saw as now enshrined in customary law but did include several that neither the *Restatement* nor Henkin's personal amendment had listed (such as a right to have governments suppress "advocacy of national, racial or religious hatred" and the right of "minorities . . . to enjoy their own culture . . . or use their own language"). Ibid., p. 20. Meanwhile, another commentator has predicted that the list will soon include "environmental protections and the right to political access . . . and other attributes of democracy." Ibid., p. 198. Australian commentators protested against the "mainstream position . . . in the United States" that "satisfies its appetite by resorting to a progressive, streamlined theory of customary law, more or less stripped of traditional practice requirement, and through this dubious operation is able to find a customary law of human rights whenever it is needed." Bruno Simma and Philip Alston, "The Sources of Human Rights Law," *Australian Yearbook of International Law*, vol. 12 (1992), p. 107.

17. A few countries did subsequently enact laws giving their courts jurisdiction to hear criminal charges against perpetrators of extreme human rights abuses in other countries. As expected, those laws were initially applied in Canada and Australia to trials of very old Nazi war criminals discovered to have been living there—and Germany did not oppose those prosecutions.

Then, in September of 1998, a Spanish judge, invoking such a law in Spain, persuaded British authorities to hold Gerneral Augusto Pinochet, former president of Chile, for extradition to

Spain, where it was proposed to try Pinochet for murders committed by his military government in Chile more than two decades earlier. A Spanish court (in rejecting the objections of other Spanish officials to the extradition request) ruled that this prosecution could be justified under "customary international law" even for murders of Chilean nationals by Chilean authorities in Chile. Neither the strong protest of the current, democratic government of Chile, nor the absence of any precedent for such a prosecution (over the protest of the defendant's home country), deterred Spanish judges from their claim that "customary international law" would support such a criminal jurisdiction in a third country as a matter of "accepted practice." The main argument of Spanish authorities for that conclusion was that most countries have now signed the UN's Genocide Convention. While the convention defines *genocide* as directed against distinct "ethnic, racial or religious groups," Spanish judges reasoned that its spirit could extend to killings directed at distinct political or ideological groups as well. And by similar reasoning, Spanish judges felt free to cite the Genocide Convention as authority for a Spanish trial, though the convention itself makes no provision for trials by other states (other than the state whose nationals have been victimized).

The ruling was a dramatic illustration of the fact that "evidence" for customary human rights law does not limit the resulting "law" to the actual scope of the evidence. The case also shows how that law can ground itself on an international consensus where none actually exists: the first British court to hear Pinochet's plea for release held, unanimously, that customary international law could not justify his arrest in Britain nor his extradition to Spain, because Spain had no rightful authority to try the former Chilean dictator for crimes committed against Chileans in Chile. Also quite revealing about the character of that "customary international human rights law" is that, amidst insistent protests from the current government of Chile, both the British and Spanish prime ministers claimed that the handling of charges against the former president of Chile was "not a political but a legal matter." So "international law" in that area is supposed to have no relevance to the foreign policies of politically accountable governments, but to operate, it seems, in its own transcendent realm.

18. See *Department of State Bulletin*, vol. 83, no. 2075 (1983), p.

7071; President Reagan's statement to that effect appears in the *Weekly Compilation of Presidential Documents*, vol. 19 (1983), p. 383.

19. The claim regarding federal preemption has been disputed. See Jack Goldsmith, "Federal Courts, Foreign Affairs, and Federalism," *Virginia Law Review*, vol. 83 (November 1997), p. 1617. But that is still a distinctly minority position.

20. Louis Henkin, "The Constitution and United States Sovereignty," *Harvard Law Review*, vol. 100 (1987), p. 875.

21. Louis Henkin, "The President and International Law," *American Journal of International Law*, vol. 80 (1986), pp. 930, 935–36; Michael J. Glennon, "Raising the *Paquete Habana:* Is Violation of Customary International Law by the Executive Unconstitutional?" *Northwestern University Law Review*, vol. 80 (1985), pp. 348–58; Jules Lobel, "The Limits of Constitutional Power: Conflicts between Foreign Policy and International Law," *Virginia Law Review*, vol. 71 (1985), pp. 1116–20.

22. Indeed, international law journals now speak of "instant customary international law." See, for example, Michael Byers, "Custom, Power, and the Rules of Customary International Law," *Michigan Journal of International Law*, vol. 17 (Fall 1995), p. 109, fn. 19, citing conventions on genocide and on peaceful uses of outer space, supposed to have passed "instantly" into customary law because no nation opposed those treaties (though, of course, no nation had any incentive to do so, because it could not readily violate those unenforceable or unviolatable treaties). See, also, Gary L. Scott and Craig L. Carr, "Multilateral Treaties and the Formation of Customary International Law," *Denver Journal of International Law and Policy*, vol. 25 (Fall 1996), p. 71, n. 33, tracing history of the phrase to articles published in the 1970s (again on the genocide and space conventions).

23. Indeed, relying on mere paper proclamations is hard to avoid, since so little in the way of "hard law" exists to determine what is actually the accepted practice of states—in the sense of obligations accepted by states as actual obligations under international law:

> Whether human rights obligations have become customary law cannot be readily answered on the basis of the usual process of customary law formation. States do not usually make claims on other States or protest violations that do

not affect their nationals. . . . Arbitral awards and international judicial decisions are also rare. . . . The arguments advanced in support of a finding that rights are a part of customary law rely on different kinds of evidence . . . [none of which] conform to the traditional criteria [for determining whether a practice has become customary law, by acceptance of states as legal obligations in actual international practice].

Oscar Schachter, "International Law in Theory and Practice," *Recueil des Cours,* vol. 178 (1982-V), pp. 334–35.

24. Louis Sohn, "Sources of International Law," *Georgia Journal of International and Comparative Law,* vol. 25 (1995–1996), p. 399.

25. Convention on Discrimination against Women, Art. 11, ¶ 1: "State parties shall take all appropriate measures to eliminate discrimination against women in the field of employment in order to ensure . . . (d) The right to equal remuneration, including benefits, and to equal treatment in respect of work of equal value." ¶ 2: "[T]o prevent discrimination against women on the grounds of marriage or maternity and to ensure their effective right to work, State parties shall take appropriate measures . . . (c) To encourage the provision of the necessary supporting social services to combine family obligations with work responsibilities and participation in public life, in particular through promoting the establishment and development of a network of childcare facilities." As of 1991 (the last year in which the UN published a survey of ratifications), that convention had been signed by 123 countries and fully ratified by 111 countries. It is apparently on the strength of that long roster of signatories that Professor Henkin concluded that the right to be free of "gender discrimination" has now entered customary international law. If the general principle enters on that basis, why not the specifics as spelled out in that very widely subscribed treaty?

26. Gordon Christensen, "Customary International Law in Domestic Court Decisions," *Georgia Journal of International and Comparative Law,* vol. 25 (1995–1996), p. 225.

27. The Third *Restatement* notes that 28 U.S.C. § 1331 gives U.S. district courts original jurisdiction "of all civil actions arising under the Constitution, laws and treaties of the United States." The *Restatement* then immediately goes on to note that the term

treaties in that context can include other kinds of international agreements, and, anyway, matters "arising under customary international law also arise under 'the laws of the United States,' since international law is 'part of our law'" (§ 111, n. 4).

28. *U.S. v. Alvarez-Machain*, 504 U.S. 655 (1992) [refusing to challenge abduction of Mexican citizens for prosecution in the United States, despite contrary international custom]; *Sale v. Haitian Ctrs. Council*, 113 S. Ct. 2549 (1994) [refusing to interfere with U.S. administration practice of turning away Haitian refugees on the seas, despite customary law indications that Refugee Convention would bar such practice]; *Mir v. Meese*, 788 F.2d 1446 (11th Cir. 1986) [refusing to challenge Justice Department practice of detaining undocumented aliens, despite indications of contrary international norms].

29. The Marshall Court ruling was *Murray v. Charming Betsy*, 6 U.S. (2 Cranch) 64 (1804) ("an act of Congress ought never to be considered to violate the law of nations if any other possible construction remains," which did, in fact, concern customary international law. The rule is still ritually invoked by federal courts. "Federal statutes ought never to be construed to violate the law of nations if any other possible construction remains." *Spiess v. C. Itoh & Co.*, 643 F.2d 353 (1981). Some commentators have challenged that interpretive rule. See Curtis Bradley, "The *Charming Betsy Canon* and Separation of Powers: Rethinking the Interpretive Role of International Law," *Georgetown Law Journal*, vol. 86 (1998), p. 479. But that is still a dissenting view.

30. "With prospects for the successful direct invocation of the UN Charter and other international human rights treaties in U.S. courts remote at present . . . international human rights law could be used more effectively by infusing its normative content into U.S. constitutional and statutory standards. . . . This 'indirect incorporation' of international human rights law continues to be a promising approach warranting greater attention and increased use by human rights advocates." Richard Lillich, "International Human Rights Law in U.S. Courts," *Journal of Transnational Law and Politics*, vol. 2 (1993), p. 19.

31. "Whatever the ethical merits or political appeal of this theory (of comparable worth), it has no standing in civil rights law." *Davidson v. Bd. of Governors, Western Illinois University*, 920 F.2d 441 (1990). See also: *American Nurses' Ass'n v. Illinois*, 783

F.2d 716 (7th Cir. 1986); *American Federation of State, County & Municipal Employees (AFSCME) v. Washington,* 770 F.2d 1401, 1407 (9th Cir. 1985); *Spaulding v. University of Washington,* 740 F.2d 686, 706–7 (9th Cir. 1984); *Lemons v. City & County of Denver,* 620 F.2d 228 (10th Cir. 1980); *Christensen v. Iowa,* 563 F.2d 353 (8th Cir. 1977).

32. Many different versions of such arguments exist. Some scholars have urged that the First Amendment be read to allow restraints on hate speech to make them compatible with international conventions requiring such restraints. Others argue that constitutional restrictions on affirmative action should be relaxed to bring the United States into accord with supposed standards of international law. Others have urged that international norms be invoked when the Constitution, by itself, does not supply a desired requirement. Even that approach can have startling consequences. In 1997 the Supreme Court struck down the Religious Freedom Restoration Act, on the grounds that none of the enumerated powers of Congress gave it the authority to impose such broad-ranging requirements on state and local governments. *City of Boerne v. Flores,* 117 S. Ct. 2157 (1997). (That act sought to require exemptions from otherwise valid laws whenever such laws imposed a "substantial burden" on religious practice that did not reflect a "compelling state interest.") Shortly afterward, a scholar argued that the act could be revived as an implementation of U.S. treaty commitments under the Covenant on Civil and Political Rights (which has vague language about religious freedom). Gerald Neuman, "The Global Dimension of RFRA," *Constitutional Commentaries,* vol. 14 (1997), p. 33.

33. In *Thompson v. Oklahoma,* 487 U.S. 815 (1988), the plurality opinion by Justice Stevens affirmed "the relevance of the views of the international community in determining whether a punishment is cruel and unusual" (p. 830, n. 31). Justice O'Connor's concurring opinion also acknowledged the relevance of international norms. Justice Scalia protested that "the views of other nations, however enlightened the Justices of this Court may think them to be, cannot be imposed upon Americans through the Constitution" (p. 868, n. 4). But only two other justices (Rehnquist and White) joined that opinion. Scalia repeated that argument, this time with three other justices, in the plurality opinion in *Standford v. Kentucky,* 492 U.S. 361 (1989), p. 369, n. 1, where the

Court upheld the constitutionality of executing an eighteen-year-old. The Court had previously taken note of the "UN Standard Minimum Rules for the Treatment of Prisoners" (a 1957 resolution of the Economic and Social Council) in *Estelle v. Gamble*, 429 U.S. 97 (1976), p. 102, but ignored those standards (when affirming a prison practice in conflict with them) in *Rhodes v. Chapman*, 452 U.S. 337 (1981).

34. Justice Blackmun, one of the most activist justices on the Court in the last generation, was alert to the possibilities. Shortly after his retirement, he gave an after-dinner address at the annual meeting of the American Society of International Law, urging the Court to pay more respectful attention to international law as a potential source of guidance for U.S. law: "Although the recent decisions of the Supreme Court do not offer much hope for the immediate future, I look forward to the day when the Supreme Court, too, will inform its opinions almost all the time with a decent respect to the opinions of mankind." "Justice Blackmun Addresses ASIL Annual Dinner," *ASIL Newsletter*, March 1994, pp. 6–7.

35. 517 U.S. 620 (1996).

36. See n. 16 supra for commentators claiming that "autonomy" rights are already part of customary international law.

37. In 1965, the Second *Restatement* noted that the domestic legal status of customary international law was "not settled" (§ 3, rep. n. 2). Yet, the Third *Restatement* reported "general agreement" that customary international law is now part of U.S. law. It cited no court rulings to that effect but simply cited as its authority an article by Chief Reporter Henkin, which had in turn cited a tentative draft for the same *Restatement*—for which Henkin himself was chief reporter. Bradley and Goldsmith, "Current Illegitimacy," p. 342, deride that as "pure bootstrapping," but the prestige of the *Restatement* is testimony to the wide sympathy for its tendencies among legal scholars.

38. The Cornell Law School, which tries to maintain a complete collection of legal periodicals, has sixty-two journals of international law published by American law schools. Not one of them existed before 1960. Of the sixty-two journals now available, eighteen have been publishing only since 1990, thirty-four only since 1980, and fifty-three since 1970. Only three were in existence before 1965, and even those appeared only in more

modest form. *The Harvard International Law Journal,* for example, was published until 1966 as the *Harvard International Law Club Journal.*

39. Bradley and Goldsmith, "Customary International Law as Federal Common Law," report that as of August 1996, 250 judges, including 189 federal judges, had participated in Aspen Institute seminars on customary international human rights law, all taught by professors (Louis Henkin, Harold Koh, and Ralph Steinhardt) sympathetic to the view that U.S. law has incorporated a customary international law of human rights. The seminars are organized by Alice Henkin, wife of Louis Henkin.

40. Meanwhile, Nadine Strossen, executive director of the American Civil Liberties Union, has written a series of articles urging that international human rights conventions be adopted as standards for rights protection in the United States. See Nadine Strossen, "U.S. Ratification of the International Bill of Rights: A Fitting Celebration of the Bicentennial of the U.S. Bill of Rights," *University of Toledo Law Review,* vol. 24 (1992), p. 203 [noting that "in certain important respects, international human rights norms are more rights-protective than the corresponding domestic-law standards"], p. 204; Strossen, "Recent U.S. and International Judicial Protection of Individual Rights: A Comparative Legal Process Analysis and Proposed Synthesis," *Hastings Law Journal,* vol. 41 (1990), p. 805; Paul Hoffman and Nadine Strossen, "Enforcing International Human Rights in the United States," in Louis Henkin and John Lawrence Hargrove, eds., *Human Rights: An Agenda for the Next Century* (1994). Paul Hoffman, previously director of the Southern California American Civil Liberties Union, now directs a litigation program on international human rights.

41. For fuller elaborations of the argument, see Jordan Paust, "Race-Based Affirmative Action and International Law," *Michigan Journal of International Law,* vol. 19 (1997), p. 659; Connie de la Vega, "Civil Rights during the 1990s: New Treat, Law Could Help Immensely," *University of Cincinnati Law Review,* vol. 65 (1997), p. 423.

42. The committee included representatives from Ecuador, Egypt, Jordan, Senegal, Serbia, Cyprus, Jamaica, and Mauritius, as well as from six countries in Western or Central Europe, from Japan, from Venezuela, and from Australia itself. Elizabeth Evatt, the Australian representative, comes from a family closely connected with the Australian Labor Party (her father having been

attorney general in a previous Australian Labor Party government), and that party was then in control of the federal government when Evatt was nominated to the Human Rights Committee.

43. The decision of the Human Rights Committee was not circulated by the United Nations but has been published in Australia: "Human Rights Committee, the Toonen Case," *Australian Law Journal*, vol. 69 (August 1995), p. 600. General background is provided in Penelope Mathew, "International Law and the Protection of Human Rights in Australia: Recent Trends," *Sydney Law Review*, vol. 17 (1995), p. 177, and subsequent developments received regular coverage in the Australian daily press. Peter Fray, "UN Rules, OK?" *Bulletin* (Sydney), October 11, 1994, pp. 18–19, traces political divisions on the issue and quotes the federal attorney general as denying that Australia would be bound, after accepting the UN Human Rights Committee's ruling on Tasmania, to then accept its ruling on an upcoming Human Rights Committee's case challenging the federal government's own policies in detaining Asian "boat people"—that is, refugees to Australia, whom the Australian Labor Party government had sought to discourage from coming and, at any rate, excluded from the work force, in possible defiance of international conventions: "The essential point is that any determination or view expressed by the HRC is an advisory view. It can't bind the actions of Australian governments." The entire episode left a bad taste in the mouth of many conservatives. When, after subsequent federal elections, the Labor Party was replaced by a conservative government, the latter refused to sign a trade treaty with the European Union until it was rewritten to expunge a standard and seemingly quite innocuous "human rights" clause ["The parties reaffirm the importance they attach to the principles of the United Nations charter and the respective democratic principles of human rights. Respect for human rights and democratic principles is the basis for the cooperation between the parties . . . and it constitutes an essential element of the agreement"]. The Australian foreign minister warned Parliament that this provision "would allow the European Commission to suspend the trade agreement if it objected to any Australian human rights policy." *Sydney Morning Herald*, December 5, 1996, p. 10.

44. In fact, presidents have signed agreements that, in recognition of sizable opposition in the Senate, were never brought to the floor for a direct vote on ratification. Thus, for example, in

1980 President Carter signed the UN Convention for the Elimination of Discrimination against Women, but the Senate took no action on his request for ratification. The Senate has taken no action in all the years since then, but it can be said (truthfully) that the Senate has not rejected that convention.

45. *Beanal v. Freeport-McMoRan,Inc,,* 969 F. Supp. 362 (E.D. La. 1997), on behalf of workers in *Indonesia; Doe v. Unicol,* 963 F. Supp. 880 (C.D. Cal. 1997), on behalf of workers in Burma; *Aguinda v. Texaco,* 850 F. Supp. 282 (S.D. N.Y. 1994), on behalf of workers in Ecuador.

46. Congress has already come very close to endorsing that position. Having previously conditioned U.S. foreign aid on satisfactory "human rights" practices, Congress enacted a statute in 1994 that directs U.S. directors of international financial institutions (principally, the International Monetary Fund and the World Bank) to "use the voice and vote of the United States" to urge those institutions to "adopt policies to encourage borrowing countries to guarantee internationally recognized worker rights"— among which it includes minimum wage standards. 108 Stat. 1634, 22 U.S.C. 1621.

47. The Torture Victim Protection Act of 1991 (106 Stat. 73) now appears at 28 U.S.C. § 1350. It was justified as a measure to implement the then recently ratified Convention against Torture and Other Cruel, Inhumane, or Degrading Treatment or Punishment, 23 I.L.M. 1027 (1983), as modified, 24 I.L.M. 535 (1985). When the Senate ratified that convention, however, it attached the usual reservations, understandings, and declarations to ensure that it would not have any effect in domestic law, without explicit, subsequent legislation. And that act is, in fact, narrower in its provisions than the Convention against Torture. Nonetheless, some commentators have cited the enactment of that measure as implicit congressional endorsement for invoking customary international norms in American courts, given that some members of Congress did express such approval in the course of debate on the Torture Victim Protection Act—even if the statute does not do so. See, for example, Ryan Goodman and Derek Jinks, *"Filartiga's* Firm Footing: International Human Rights and Federal Common Law," *Fordham Law Review,* vol. 66 (1997), p. 514, and the critical response from Bradley and Goldsmith, "Current Illegitimacy," pp. 363–69.

Chapter 6: Preserving the Domestic Character of Domestic Affairs

1. Debate in the Virginia Ratifying Convention, J. Elliott, ed., *Debates on the Adoption of the Federal Constitution*, 2d ed., vol. 3 (1888), pp. 513–14.

2. "The power of making treaties . . . relates to war, peace and commerce." *The Federalist* No. 64 (Clinton Rossiter, ed., Mentor, NAL Penguin, 1961), p. 390.

3. "With regard to their power of making treaties, it is of importance, that it should be very seldom exercised. . . . [I]t will be but once in a number of years that a single treaty will come before the senate." James Wilson, "Summation and Final Rebuttal" at Pennsylvania Ratifying Convention, B. Bailyn, ed., *Debate on the Constitution*, vol. 1 (Library of America, 1993), p. 851.

4. See, for example, the statement of Rep. James Hillhouse that a treaty must relate "to objects within the province of the Treaty-making power, a power which is not unlimited. . . . The objects upon which it can operate are understood and well defined, and if the Treaty-making power were to embrace other objects, their doings would have no more binding force than if the Legislature were to assume and exercise judicial powers under the name of Legislation." *Annals of Congress*, vol. 5, column 660. In the same debate, Theodore Sedgwick said: "The power of treating between independent nations might be classed under the following heads: 1. To compose and adjust differences, whether to terminate or to prevent war. 2. To form contracts for mutual security or defence; or to make Treaties, offensive or defensive. 3. To regulate an intercourse for mutual benefit, or to form Treaties of commerce," ibid., 515). Shortly after that debate, Jefferson's *Manual of Parliamentary Practice* stipulated that treaties must "concern the foreign nation, party to the contract" and "only those objects which are usually regulated by treaty." Jefferson, like other advocates in the Founding era, suggested as well that the treaty power is no broader than the enumerated powers or, in other words, is not, in itself, an enumerated power, which seems, at the least, a very unlikely interpretation, one that was not, in fact, followed even in the first decades of federal diplomacy, and not one embraced even by many commentators who agreed that the treaty power must be limited in other respects.

5. The quoted phrase is from *Geofroy v. Riggs,* 133 U.S. 258 (1890), p. 267. It is echoed (or prefigured) both in other Court rulings and in much commentary. For example, in *Holmes v. Jennison,* 39 U.S. (14 Pet.) 540 (1840), p. 569, the Court held that treaties may reach "all those subjects, which in the ordinary intercourse of nations had usually been made subjects of negotiation and treaty." In *Holden v. Joy,* 84 U.S. (17 Wall.) 211 (1872), p. 243, the Court held that treaties may deal with "all those objects which in the intercourse of nations, had usually been regarded as the proper subject of negotiation and treaty, if not inconsistent with the nature of our government." And in *Santovincenzo v. Egan,* 284 U.S. 30 (1931), p. 40, the Court held that the treaty power extends to "all subjects that properly pertain to our foreign relations." Among commentators, William Rawle, *A View of the Constitution of the United States* (P.H. Nicklin, 1829), observed that the treaty power is limited to subjects "which properly arise from intercourse with foreign nations," which he specified as "peace, alliance, commerce, neutrality and others of a similar nature," pp. 57–58. Nearly a century later, the same view was still endorsed by W. W. Willoughby, *The Constitutional Law of the United States* (Baker, Voorhis, 1910), pp. 66–67: "To accept [a plenary treaty power] would be at once to overturn the long line of decisions that have held the United States Government to be one of limited, enumerated powers." Other examples are surveyed in Curtis A. Bradley, "The Treaty Power and American Federalism," *Michigan Law Review,* vol. 97, November 1998, from which those examples were drawn.

6. *U.S. v. Lopez,* 514 U.S. 549 (1995); *City of Boerne v. Flores,* 117 S. Ct. 2157 (1997).

7. The point was put this way some sixty years ago:

> If the Federal Government should seek to use the treaty-making power as a mask for regulating internal affairs . . . the way is still open for the courts to [rule that] . . . that which bears the name of a treaty . . . may not always be a treaty. . . . From the earliest days of our Government, those who have considered the problem have been struck by the apparent anomaly of permitting the president and part of the Senate ["It will be noted that Art. II, sec. 2, cl. 2 of the Constitution requires the advice and consent of only two-thirds of the senators *present.*"] plus some Indian chief or

foreign prince to accomplish that which the president,
Senate and House of Representatives . . . cannot do.

Ernest F. Fiedler and Ralph H. Dwan, "The Extent of the Treaty-
Making Power," *Georgetown Law Journal,* vol. 28 (1939), p. 195.

8. The argument has long been made—starting with authorities as eminent as Thomas Jefferson—that the treaty power extends no further than the other powers of Congress enumerated
in Article I, Sec. 8. The Supreme Court repudiated that view in
Missouri v. Holland, 252 U.S. 416 (1920), holding that Congress
could enact protective measures for migratory birds pursuant to
a treaty with Canada, even though a similar statute had earlier
been struck down, as in excess of federal power, when not tied to
a treaty. Long before that, court rulings had embraced treaties
on matters (such as inheritance and land ownership) that would
not otherwise have been proper subjects of federal regulation.
But the argument in the text is, in any case, different. The treaty
power is a distinct power, which may extend beyond other enumerated powers in some respects or in some contexts. Still, the
treaty power is not unlimited as to content. The power must be
limited to matters of genuinely international concern—as the
traditional sources held. That doctrine will not ensure that the
states are never restricted by treaty, nor even that treaties never
restrict the states more than federal statutes might do. But it does,
at least, hold restrictions under the treaty power to proper occa-
sions for such restriction.

9. In *United States v. Lopez,* 514 U.S. 549 (1995), the Court
rejected the Gun Free School Zone Act on the ground that the
statute "by its terms has nothing to do with 'commerce' or any
sort of economic enterprise, however broadly one might define
those terms (p. 561)." The Court acknowledged that past decisions had endorsed regulation of intrastate activity, but only where
such activity had some reasonably direct impact on interstate commerce and was necessary to regulate the interstate matter in question. But in that case, the Court held that the gun-control measure was

> not an essential part of a larger regulation of economic
> activity, in which the regulatory scheme could be under-
> cut unless the intrastate activity were regulated. It cannot,
> therefore, be sustained under our cases upholding regula-

tions of activities that arise out of or are connected with a commercial transaction, which viewed in the aggregate, substantially affects interstate commerce (p. 561).

10. Chief Justice Hughes in a 1929 address on international commitments (*Proceedings of the American Society of International Law*, vol. 23 (1929), p. 194) pointed toward just that sort of analysis when he suggested that properly international matters might be gauged by analogy with properly "interstate" matters under the Commerce Clause jurisprudence of that era. The Court no longer enforces limits on the Commerce Clause with the same rigor as it did then. Still, one might argue that, on the basis of both history and structure, the border-crossing test should be applied more rigorously against treaties than against federal legislation. Where the Framers repeatedly indicated that treaties would be unusual, they made no such claims about federal legislation. Moreover, the federal government does remain accountable in fundamental ways, even if it is not held within the most strictly conceived limits of the Commerce Clause. The international system is in no way comparably accountable, so that much more is at stake when power is transferred to treaty makers (bargaining with foreign governments) than when extra powers are conceded to Congress, acting on its own.

11. *U.S. v. Lopez*, 514 U.S. 549 (1995). The definitional point—that *commerce* must involve economic exchange, buying and selling, as the ordinary meaning of the term implies—was particularly stressed in concurring opinions by Justices Kennedy and Thomas.

12. *The Federalist* No. 64 (Jay), Rossiter, ed., p. 394; No. 75 (Hamilton), p. 450 (emphasis in original). To the same effect was James Wilson's "Summation and Final Rebuttal" at the Pennsylvania Ratifying Convention: "[T]reaties, sir, are truly contracts or compacts, between the different states, nations or princes, who find it convenient or necessary to enter into them." Bailyn, *Debate on the Constitution*, vol. 1, p. 844.

13. Even the Third *Restatement* suggests something of the sort. It takes note of the statement of Chief Justice Hughes in 1929 that the treaty power would properly extend only to matters "relating to foreign affairs" and not to matters "which did not pertain to our external relations." It then speculates that "Hughes's statement may have implied only that an international agreement of the United States must be a bona fide agreement with another

state, serving a foreign policy interest or purpose of the United States. That requirement may well be implied in the word 'treaty' or 'agreement' as used in international law and the United States Constitution." But stated so loosely, it suggests that anything that the president chooses to characterize as a "foreign policy interest or purpose" is so and sufficiently so for a treaty. The argument in the text presumes that something more is required—an actual exchange in which the other party makes some concession or commitment in a context in which there is some reasonable expectation that it can be held to that or else the United States can withdraw from its own commitment. Domestic contracts, it is true, are regarded as valid even when the consideration from one side is altogether trifling. But domestic contracts have a reliable court system to enforce them. No general counterpart exists in international law. Even the International Court of Justice accepts only those cases in which both parties have agreed to submit to its jurisdiction, so that it is really more of an arbitration panel than a court. Moreover, much less is at stake in private contracts than in international treaties. Parties to private contracts are presumed to know their own interests and to act on them. In an international treaty, the government speaks for the citizenry, which is why we have constitutional restraints on government. A treaty is always, to some extent, a restriction on what the people could seek in the absence of a treaty, since a treaty makes a commitment to another party. Given those basic characteristics of treaties, it is reasonable to assume that the term "treaty" implies something more stringent than what might be required for a private contract. At the extreme, the point is easy to grasp. Imagine a "treaty" by which the United States promised Canada that the United States would enact federal legislation to change U.S. divorce law (otherwise a matter reserved to the states), in return for which Canada promised to let the United States do so (or not to criticize it for doing so). Almost no one would pretend that this is a valid exercise of the treaty power. How much genuine reciprocity must be involved—how much, that is, the other party must return something of value and do so in a way that is reliably tied to American commitments in the treaty—can be disputed. But the principle seems fundamental. And taken seriously, it has a good deal more force than vague references to "foreign policy interests."

14. See *Ware v. Hylton*, 3 Dall. 242. Treaties to that effect were

signed in the course of the nineteenth century with France, Russia, Austria, Naples, most of the German states, Mexico, and most of the South American states.

15. To be sure, not every international agreement that involves mutual concessions can be resolved into neatly divisible exchanges in quite that way. Conservation agreements on deep sea fishing or agreements on airport security cannot be enforced by direct withdrawal of reciprocity. The United States cannot reduce its security precautions at Kennedy Airport in New York simply to punish Greece for failing to maintain proper precautions in Athens. Canada cannot punish Spain for overfishing in the waters off Newfoundland simply by overfishing itself. But some concessions can be readily tied to others that are divisible: if Greece fails in its obligation to provide proper airport security, we can deny planes from Athens the right to land at American airports. Other agreements—as with fishing agreements—do sometimes break down and require unilateral responses: Canada imposed national controls in a 200-mile economic zone. But where there is no meaningful provision for reciprocity, good grounds exist to question whether a commitment is genuinely international or simply a series of parallel national policies, masquerading as international agreements.

16. "It is an established doctrine on the subject of treaties that all articles are mutually conditions of each other; that a breach of any one article is a breach of the whole treaty; and that a breach, committed by either of the parties, absolves the others [sic], and authorizes them, if they please, to pronounce the compact null and void." *The Federalist* No. 43 (Rossiter, ed., p. 280).

17. Henkin, "Human Rights and State Sovereignty," *Georgia Journal of International and Comparative Law*, vol. 25 (1995–1996), pp. 39, 36.

18. The International Court of Justice recognized that point as far back as 1951 in its advisory opinion on whether states ratifying the new Convention on Genocide could make highly restrictive reservations (Advisory Opinion of the International Court of Justice, Reservations to the Genocide Convention, I.C.J. Rep. 15, 21). Some nations objected to that practice by others, and the UN asked the ICJ to rule on the status of such partial ratifications. By traditional doctrine, as the court acknowledged, a nation that fully ratified all the terms of a multilateral convention would be entitled to deny any obligations (under that conven-

tion) to a nation that insisted on its own highly restrictive or idiosyncratic reservations to that convention. It would not be an actual agreement if one party bound itself fully while another gave itself the right to reform its part of the agreement unilaterally. But the court concluded that the special character and purpose of the Genocide Convention required a distinctive, new approach, so all ratifying nations—those that ratified in full and those that ratified only with restrictive reservations—should be considered, at least from an international perspective, genuine parties to the convention. The opinion is noted with approval in the Third *Restatement*, § 313, reporter's note 1.

19. Henkin, "Human Rights and State Sovereignty," *Georgia Journal of International and Comparative Law*, vol. 25 (1995–1996), pp. 38–39. The point is elaborated in Henkin's book, *International Law: Politics and Values* (1995), which also speaks of an "international constitutional law" (p. 31). Henkin's point is that the law of human rights is no longer seen to depend on the particularized consent of particular nations. Instead, successive treaties have (in his view) given international human rights law a momentum that is now independent of state policy: instead of reflecting the consent of states (as in the old conception of customary law or treaties), the new international law of human rights is, he claims, a "reflection of the [international] system's steady drift toward human values. . . . It is perhaps the only instance of a new body of international law born and grown in response to an idea, to public opinion—domestic and international opinion" ("Human Rights and State Sovereignty," p. 36).

20. A notable early example is *Mayor of New Orleans v. U.S.*, 10 Pet. 662 (1836), restricting application of governing powers seemingly transferred to the federal government by the treaty with France ceding the Louisiana Territory to the United States.

21. See, for example, *Bullfrog Films, Inc. v. Wick*, 847 F.2d. 502 (9th Cir. 1988), rejecting, as contrary to the First Amendment, the United States' implementing regulations for a multilateral treaty providing tariff exemptions for a certain category of films.

22. Harold Koh, *The National Security Constitution* (Yale University Press, 1990), ch. 6, analyzes the pattern at some length.

23. The Bush administration does not seem to have doubted that competent lawyers might still make a reasonable case for the president's authority to act without formal approval from Congress. Rather, the concern was that, should the war prove to be

costly and protracted, the president would be extremely exposed and vulnerable if he could not remind congressional critics that Congress itself had given its own formal endorsement for the war. It would be wrong, however, to see the first concern as "legal" and the second as "political." Looking back on the Vietnam experience, President Bush drew the lesson that the country would not give full support to a war if it were seen as merely a presidential war, rather than a truly national war endorsed by Congress. That is not merely a "political" analysis but a constitutional one: it is based on a rather formal but still fundamental notion of how the country operates.

24. Louis Fisher, *Presidential War Power* (University Press of Kansas, 1995), pp. 114–33.

25. Many supporters of the Bricker Amendment were southern representatives, fearful that international human rights treaties would be invoked against racial segregation laws in the South. But the American Bar Association voiced objections on other grounds, and the critics included quite reputable scholars and jurists. See, for example, George Finch, "The Need to Restrain the Treaty Making Power of the United States within Constitutional Limits," *American Journal of International Law*, vol. 48 (1954), p. 57. Finch was a former editor of that leading American journal on international law. Both the Genocide Convention and what later became the Covenant on Civil and Political Rights include requirements that government suppress forms of speech (hate speech in the one case and "propaganda for war" in the other), and such requirements would probably be in violation of the First Amendment. The Supreme Court's subsequent decision in *Reid v. Covert* suggests that the First Amendment would prevail over treaty requirements, in any case. But it is worth noting that arguments for an accommodating approach to international organizations (as in Henkin's *Foreign Affairs and the Constitution;* see, for example, remarks quoted in chap. 4, n. 7) more or less openly assume that the Constitution can be reinterpreted to suit the needs of a new era, and some international law scholars have argued, in the same way, that the First Amendment and other provisions of the Bill of Rights should be reinterpreted to accommodate full U.S. compliance with human rights conventions. See, for example, Jordan Paust, "Rereading the First Amendment in Light of Treaties Proscribing Incitement to Racial Discrimination or Hostility," *Rutgers Law Review,* vol. 43 (1991), p. 565.

Chapter 7: Chasing Gobal Warming or Chilling Global Trade?

1. Art. 3, Par. 4.

2. Art. 12.

3. It is true, of course, that greenhouse gases do drift across borders. The constitutional problem is that the gases, in themselves, do no direct or immediate harm. What the treaty proposes to regulate is not actual cross-border currents of gas, but emissions within each country. And the warming trend, if it occurs, cannot be traced to any particular country's emissions. In *U.S. v. Lopez*, the Justice Department tried to defend the Gun Free School Zone Act on the grounds that more guns in schools might lead to more violence, which might lead to less learning by students, which might make those students less productive or employable when they grow up, which might, in the end, hurt the economy on a scale that would affect interstate transactions. The majority of the Supreme Court dismissed the argument as built on a chain of premises so tenuous that it could be used to justify anything, thereby converting a limited power to regulate interstate commerce into a general power to regulate everything. ("To uphold the Government's contentions here, we would have to pile inference upon inference in a manner that would bid fair to convert congressional authority under the Commerce Clause to a general police power of the sort retained by the States,"*U.S. v. Lopez* 514 U.S. 549, p. 567.) The Kyoto Protocol presents a similar analytic problem. Many observers, for example, hold that international disparities in wealth may lead to increasingly dangerous resentment in other countries, which might threaten world peace by the end of the next century. Would that justify a treaty by which the United States commits itself to make massive wealth transfers to other countries today? Even if the treaty proposes to donate a specified fraction of revenue earned from foreign trade, no connection exists between the money that crosses borders and the redistributive donation to other countries. The treaty is not in any genuine sense about regulating something that crosses borders.

4. The International Energy Authority has calculated that in 1990, OECD countries produced 10,126 million metric tons (Mt) of energy-related carbon-dioxide emissions (or 48.7 percent of the world total). Less developed countries (rest of the world— exclusive of OECD and countries of Central/Eastern Europe/

former Soviet Union) produced 6,227 Mt of CO_2 (30 percent of the world total). If present trends continued (that is, without any effect from Kyoto commitments), the IEA calculates that by 2010, CO_2 emissions would increase by 26 percent for OECD countries—to reach 12,738 Mt—but emissions from less-developed countries would more than double to 14,084 (45.6 percent of the world total by then, versus 41.1 percent for OECD countries). Figures are from IEA, *World Energy Outlook* (1996 ed.). If by 2010, OECD countries actually did manage to reduce their CO_2 emissions by 8 percent below 1990 levels (as the Kyoto Protocol contemplates), that decrease would represent a mere 10 percent of the increase in emissions from less-developed countries: the extra emissions from less-developed countries, in other words, would be nearly ten times larger than the reductions accomplished by OECD countries—and less-developed countries would account for some 47 percent of world output of CO_2, nearly the share of global emissions that the OECD countries now produce.

5. The point has been argued quite cogently by an American economist:

> [We might] do more to protect the Indian population of 2050 and 2075, for example, from climate change by accelerating economic development in India now than by slowing down climate change itself. . . . [We might focus on] accelerating development [now] so that if and when climate change comes about, people will be much less vulnerable to the damage that might occur.

Thomas Schelling, *Costs and Benefits of Greenhouse Gas Reduction* (AEI Press 1998), p. 16. Schelling notes that rich countries are much better able to cope with climatic variation, among other reasons because agriculture and other weather-related activities are a so much smaller portion of their overall economies. Besides, devoting extensive resources to climate control today represents, in effect, a wealth transfer from today's poor to their much more affluent grandchildren:

> If today we had foreign aid to divide between Bangladesh and Singapore, who would give any to Singapore? But if many developing countries in fifty or seventy-five years will be close to Singapore's level of development now, then it

seems backwards to avoid promoting economic development around the world today and focusing on slowing down
climate change because of the good it will do for future
generations.

6. A well-considered argument for the former is offered in
Richard Cooper, "Why Kyoto Won't Work," *Foreign Affairs*, March/
April 1998, which concedes that global warming may be a problem and proposes a system of international carbon taxes as a more
feasible alternative to the Kyoto system. Readers may be quite
persuaded by Cooper's objections to the feasibility of the Kyoto
scheme and then conclude that his alternate scheme of international taxation remains subject to the same sorts of objections.

7. North American Agreement on Environmental Cooperation, reprinted in 32 I.L.M. 1480 (1993); North American Agreement on Labor Cooperation, reprinted in 32 I.L.M. 1499 (1993).

8. In fact, the first submission to the new North American
Commission on Environmental Cooperation (based in Montreal)
was from a U.S. environmental advocacy group, protesting that
the Republicans in Congress had suspended the application of
the Endangered Species Act in forest lands in the Pacific North-
west (pending resolution of a dispute between logging companies and defenders of the endangered spotted owl). The commission decided that this constituted a (permissible) change in
the law rather than a (prohibited) act of nonenforcement.
Biodiversity Legal Foundation et al., Case No. SEM-95-001 (June 30,
1995) (on file with the Environmental Secretariat and available
at http://www.cec.org, under Citizen Submissions—Article 14,
Registry of Submissions). Some observers see such decisions as
reflecting a calculated policy of avoiding controversy, until the
commission's authority is better established: "The Commission
has been extremely prudent, some would say too prudent, in its
approach to responding to complaints and to conducting inquir-
ies into complaints." A. L. C. de Mestral, "The Significance of the
NAFTA Side Agreements," *Arizona Journal of International and
Comparative Law*, vol. 15 (Winter 1998), p. 169. The implications
for the longer term remain unclear.

9. The dispute over the side accords came to a head when
the Clinton administration sought fast-track authorization to
negotiate Chile's entry into NAFTA in 1995. Republicans refused
to authorize negotiations on the expansion or extension of envi-

ronmental and labor side accords. The administration—and many labor and environmental advocates in Congress—insisted that NAFTA could not be expanded without extending the side accords. So there was no fast-track authorization, and Chile eventually negotiated a separate agreement with Canada. Talk of restarting negotiations on NAFTA expansion in the summer of 1998 was immediately caught up in the same issue, with the Clinton administration's continuing to insist on the importance of labor and environmental agreements. Some journalists speculated that the administration was seeking to win over liberals in Congress to support of trade liberalization by promising more ambitious environmental and labor accords. See Paul Magnusson, "Clinton's Trade Crusade," *BusinessWeek*, June 8, 1998, p. 34. In fact, when fast-track authorization came to a vote in the House of Representatives at the end of September 1998, it was defeated by 242–180, with 171 Democrats and 71 Republicans voting against a proposal that specifically excluded any negotiation on labor or environmental standards. Why did Congress defeat that authorization? According to the *Economist*, the defeat occurred "[i]n essence, because Congress is deeply divided over what a fast-track bill should say about labour standards and the environment. Most Republicans think that trade should not be linked to these issues at all. Most Democrats think it should." "Slow Road to Fast Track," *Economist*, Oct. 3, 1998, p. S32.

10. Addressing a WTO meeting, President Clinton said:

> We must do more to ensure that spirited economic competition among nations never becomes a race to the bottom—in environmental protections, consumer protections, or labor standards. Without such a strategy, we cannot build the necessary public support for continued expansion of trade. I will work to ensure that the WTO and other international institutions are more responsive to labor, the environment, consumers, and other interests so that we can build the public confidence we need in our trade expansion initiatives.

Statement of the Conclusion of the World Trade Organization Meeting, May 20, 1998, *Weekly Compilation of Presidential Documents,* vol. 34, p. 934. For a more candid exposition of labor's agenda, see Howard Wachtel, "Labor's Stake in the WTO," *American Prospect* (March–April 1998). Still the most comprehensive argument for incorporating environmental standards into the WTO is Daniel Esty, *Greening the GATT: Trade, Environment, and the Future* (Institute for International Economics, 1994).

11. For a survey of negotiating problems in establishing international environmental standards, where there is somewhat more agreement that *something* should be done, see Thomas J. Schoenbaum, "International Trade and Protection of the Environment: The Continuing Search for Reconciliation," *American Journal of International Law*, vol. 91 (1997), p. 268.

Chapter 8: American Ideals in a Nonideal World

1. Locke explains that transferring legislative power to a foreign authority will necessarily dissolve the government: "[F]or the end why people entered into society being to be preserved one intire, free, independent society, to be governed by its own laws; this is lost, whenever they are given up into the power of another" (*Second Treatise*, § 217).

2. "The major premise [of the Declaration's argument for independence] . . . is that every people has a right to make and unmake its own government; the minor premise is that the Americans are a 'people' in this sense. . . . The minor premise is . . . not explicitly stated. . . . To have stated it explicitly would perhaps have been to bring into too glaring a light certain incongruities between the assumed premise and the known historical facts." Carl Becker, *The Declaration of Independence* (New York: Vintage, 1958), pp. 203–4.

3. It is true, of course, that the United States has never been a simple democracy, that it has always sought to maintain a system of checks and balances in its governmental scheme. But that fact does not blunt the underlying point. Checks and balances only work because the separate and competing branches of the government share an underlying accountability to the whole, to the Constitution of the whole, and ultimately to the people as a whole. That was the argument of *The Federalist*—that the naturally weaker organs, like the Senate or the judiciary, could prevail against the seemingly stronger parts of the government by appealing to constitutional principles or public regard for their integrity. (See, for example, No. 63, the Senate; No. 73, executive veto; No. 78, judicial review). Our historical experience, in

fact, is that disputes among the different branches of government have rarely been pressed to destructive extremes. Despite some bitter disputes about defense policy, for example, the record of the American government in protecting American security interests looks altogether admirable compared with the record of the UN Security Council, which is most of the time deliberating on how to protect *some other country's* security.

4. Of course, there is some tension between insistence on individual rights and a strong version of sovereignty, understood as (in Blackstone's words) "a supreme, irresistible, absolute, uncontrolled authority"(*Commentaries*, bk. 1, Introduction, § 2). But a natural affinity also exists between natural rights theories and claims about national sovereignty, which can be readily traced through European texts invoked by the American Founders as well as in writings of the Founders themselves. Locke, for example, says that men accept limits on their natural rights when they agree to form a distinct political society—but each independent nation thus remains in a state of nature with every other. The rights of nations are then a kind of projection of the rights of individuals. The independence of nations reflects the primal or fundamental independence of individuals. The natural rights argument assumed that nations could be thought of as special undertakings—a pooling of rights for some purposes but not others. It simply does not follow that because one agrees to share in some matters, one agrees to share more extensively with more distant people. No one who owns stock in a corporation shrugs off wasteful corporate practices because, as a stockholder, he is already sharing his investment with many other stockholders.

True, the natural rights emphasis of the Founding Fathers implies that governments are viewed with some distrust. But the point is that authorities outside one's government are viewed with even more distrust. One's own government can be, at least to some degree and in some sense, accountable. What is outside is not even accountable. So the premise of distrust of authority, if it is at odds with extreme forms of nationalism or with unlimited domestic authority, remains even more at odds with an internationalism that breaks with constitutional forms.

5. "A major intellectual requirement of our time is to rethink the question of sovereignty—not to weaken its essence, which is crucial to international security and cooperation, but to

recognize that it may take more than one form and perform more than one function." Boutros Boutros-Ghali, "Empowering the United Nations," *Foreign Affairs*, vol. 71 (Winter 1992–1993), p. 99.

6. Those who can imagine such a law's going forward without challenge should consider what happened when the Reagan administration simply agreed to exchange ambassadors with the Vatican. Americans United for Separation of Church and State promptly challenged that diplomatic initiative in a lawsuit. The challenge was ultimately rejected in *Americans United for Separation v. Ronald Reagan*, 607 F. Supp. 747 (1985)—but on jurisdictional grounds.

7. At least under the currently prevailing doctrines, the challenge might very well succeed in the courts. See *Larkin v. Grendel's Den*, 459 U.S. 116 (1982), overturning, as violation of the Establishment Clause of the First Amendment, a local ordinance prohibiting operation of bars or restaurants serving liquor within a specified distance of a church, unless the church gives permission. See also *Board of Education of Kiryas Joel v. Grumet*, 512 U.S. 687 (1994), holding that the First Amendment prohibits operation of a school board by a village whose boundaries coincide with residence patterns of a particular Hasidic sect.

8. Apart from conspiracy theorists in the John Birch Society, serious figures also raised alarms in the 1950s—in extremely impassioned terms. For example, Frank Holman, former president of the American Bar Association, former law school dean, and former Rhodes scholar, warned that "[t]he Internationalists in this country and elsewhere really propose to use the United Nations and the treaty process as a lawmaking process to change the domestic laws and even the Government of the United States and to establish a World Government along socialistic lines." *The Year of Victory* (Argus Press, 1955), p. 4. Holman's warnings against the ambitions of the UN were provoked by the UN's convention against genocide, which the Eisenhower administration—and its next four successors—declined to submit to the Senate. One of the characteristic contemporary counterparts of such works is Cliff Kincaid, *Global Bondage: The UN Plan to Rule the World* (Huntington House Publishers, 1995), a book distributed by the same publisher that distributes works purporting to establish President Clinton's responsibility for various nefarious crimes, such as the

murder of White House Counsel Vince Foster. For the local coun-
terpart of that outlook, consider: "Peace Site Rejected in
McGregor, Minn.; Some Wary of World-Law Goal," Minneapolis
Star Tribune, November 25, 1996, p. 1B:

> Discomfort with the concept of world government led
> school board members in McGregor, Minn. to vote last week
> against naming their school district the 150th International
> Peace Site in Minnesota. Some board members said they
> weren't opposed to peace, but were wary of one goal advo-
> cated by founders and participants in the Peace Site pro-
> gram: "Working toward world law with justice through a
> strong, effective United Nations." Although it is only a small
> part of the program, the world-law idea is seen by some as
> a threat to U.S. sovereignty. Dissenters worry that if the
> United Nations is made more powerful, it might claim the
> right to invade any country, including the United States,
> in the event of disagreement.

About the Author

JEREMY RABKIN is a professor in the Department of Government at Cornell University, where he teaches American constitutional law, international law, and the history of political thought. He is also an adjunct scholar of the American Enterprise Institute. He published a monograph with the Competitive Enterprise Institute on UN supervision of public parks in American territory and presented congressional testimony of behalf of the American Land Sovereignty Act. Mr. Rabkin's article "Grotius, Vattel, and Locke: An Older View of Liberalism and Nationality" appeared in the spring 1997 issue of the *Review of Politics.* He also coedited the AEI volume *The Fettered Presidency: Legal Constraints on the Executive Branch* (1989). He received his B.A. from Cornell University and his Ph.D. in political science from Harvard University.

AEI STUDIES ON GLOBAL ENVIRONMENTAL POLICY
John R. Bolton and Robert W. Hahn, Series Editors

COSTS AND BENEFITS OF GREENHOUSE GAS REDUCTION
Thomas C. Schelling

THE ECONOMICS AND POLITICS OF CLIMATE CHANGE
Robert W. Hahn

MAKING ENVIRONMENTAL POLICY: TWO VIEWS
Irwin M. Stelzer and Paul R. Portney

WHY SOVEREIGNTY MATTERS
Jeremy Rabkin